To Aunty & Uncle
Christmas 1972
Joy & Reg.

the treasury of
BIRDS

the treasury of
BIRDS

Contributors

Whitney and Karen Eastman
Malcolm Ellis
Dr John Sparks

Ian Prestt
John Burton
David Saunders

Octopus Books Limited
London · New York · Sydney · Hong Kong

First Published 1972 by
Octopus Books Limited
30 Bouverie Street, London E.C.4

ISBN 7064 0013 5
© 1972 Octopus Books Limited

Filmset by Filmtype Services Limited,
Scarborough, England
Printed in Hong Kong

Contents

European birds

JOHN BURTON

Britain and Europe are part of the region known to zoologists as the Palearctic. This region also includes North Africa and most of Asia except India and the area south and east, roughly in a line with the Himalayas. The rest of the world is divided into similar regions on the basis that the birds and other animals within each region share certain affinities. They tend to be restricted to certain areas, though within the regions sub-regions can be recognized.

The type of bird found in any particular place depends to a large extent on the habitat. The most noticeable feature of the European landscape is the effect that man has had on it. Vast areas, once primeval forest, have been cleared; the grasslands and steppes have been planted with corn; marshes and swamps have been drained and everywhere cities and towns are spreading across the countryside. What effect does all this have on the birds? Many species just cannot survive the changes, though some others benefit and flourish.

One of the most successful and ubiquitous of European birds is the Starling. It is an extremely handsome bird and would probably be held in much higher regard were it not so common. Yet only 150 years ago it was a rare bird in many parts of Britain and Europe. Undoubtedly its ability to make use of an ever increasing amount of food, both from refuse and from the larger areas of agricultural land, together with a readiness to make use of man's buildings for nest sites has contributed a great deal towards its success. Another remarkable change in the starling's habits, which has also taken place during the last 150 years or so, is the formation of town roosts. Visitors to London will have seen the vast flocks of starlings which wheel around Trafalgar Square and the Westminster area at dusk, before settling down to roost on the ledges and window-sills of the surrounding buildings. Similar roosts are found in many other large cities – the largest roosts in Britain are those in Glasgow and Bradford, with over 50,000 birds roosting in each city at times.

Another bird closely associated with towns is the House Sparrow – it even takes its name from its habitat. In fact over the past fifty years or so the house sparrow has probably declined in most of the larger towns, since they were mainly dependent on the spillage from the nose-bags of horses for their food supply – as the numbers of horses declined so did those of the house sparrow. But although numbers may have dropped slightly in the towns the house sparrow is still one of the most successful of European birds.

The sparrows are related to the weavers, a family mainly found in Africa. There are two groups of sparrows and several sub-species all

A Willow Warbler singing its attractive song. They are difficult birds to see, but their song is easily recognized.

A House Martin and its two young sitting beside their nest. Very fast and graceful in the air as they swoop and dive after insects, they are friendly and sociable birds and relatively unafraid of humans. They often rear two broods a summer, the young of the first helping to feed the second brood, and their constant chattering and twittering is a cheerful sound under the eaves of many houses and barns.

of which are closely related. The Spanish Sparrow, which is much more widespread than its name suggests and is also found in the Balkans, Asia Minor and the Middle East, and the Italian Sparrow are both related to the house sparrow and very similar in appearance. There are several other distinct types of house sparrow – such as the migratory forms from Afghanistan and the smaller brighter coloured birds of India.

This all indicates that the house sparrow is actively evolving and has very successfully adapted to the environment created by man. Wherever man has gone and the house sparrow has managed to get a

foothold, it has usually managed to colonize. The speed at which the process of colonization takes place is well illustrated by the story of its spread in North America – the house sparrow first gained a foothold in the 1860s and by 1900 had colonized most of the U.S.A.

As a group, the martins, swallows and swifts (the latter are, in fact, unrelated but superficially similar in appearance and habits) have often found ways of co-habiting with man. The Crag Martin of southern Europe is the only species which does not make extensive use of man-made sites for nesting. House martins – like the sparrows – have a name which reflects their long association with buildings; nowadays it is quite rare to find a colony nesting on a cliff, the habitat to which they were presumably at one time restricted. They usually build their mud nest between the eaves and wall of a house, but they also build under balconies on large blocks of flats and some very large colonies have been recorded under bridges.

Sand martins utilize man-made habitats such as sand-pits, railway and road embankments where they excavate their nesting tunnels. In some places they even nest in drain pipes – why go to all the bother of digging a tunnel when man will do it for you? The swallow rarely nests away from buildings, but prefers a rather more rural habitat, nesting in farm buildings and ruins.

The Red-rumped Swallow is less widespread than most of its relatives, only being found in Spain and the Balkans, but they too make their nests on buildings and bridges as well as cliff-faces. The nest of the red-rumped swallow is a rather sock-like construction, and some of these nests were the origin of one of

the most exciting ornithological finds in recent years, when four pairs of African White-rumped Swifts were discovered nesting in the disused nests of red-rumped swallows in the Sierra de la Plata in southern Spain, in 1966. Until that time the nearest known breeding colonies of the African white-rumped swifts were south of the Sahara.

The swifts are a predominately tropical group of birds; those species which nest in northern Europe winter south of the Sahara and may in fact only spend a quarter of the year on the breeding grounds. The most widely distributed species in Europe is the common swift, which is found almost as far north as the Arctic circle. The larger and more handsomely marked Alpine Swift is only found in southern Europe, not extending much further north than Switzerland; whilst the Pallid Swift, which is extremely difficult to distinguish from the common swift, has an even more restricted range. The swifts have all, to a greater or lesser extent, adapted themselves to a man-made environment and often

nest in large colonies in church towers or beneath the roofs of houses.

The Black Redstart is another bird which has adapted itself to an urban life and their colonization of London after the blitz in 1941 is one of the great ornithological surprises. Who would have expected a bird as rare as the black redstart to make its stronghold in the heart of a city? It was originally a bird of rocky hill-sides, and is still one of Britain's rarest breeding birds, though the largest concentration is still around London. The bombed sites around St Paul's Cathedral and the Cripplegate area, where they first established themselves, have now been built over but the black redstarts have managed to adapt to a new habitat – an even more unlikely situation – on power stations and similar industrial sites. In France and other parts of western Europe they are often to be seen around cathedrals and churches, and it would seem that to some birds the differences between a rocky cliff and a bombed site, power station or

A Crag Martin lining its nest, which is built on a cliff-face. These are more southerly breeders than the House Martins and are found mainly in Spain and along the Mediterranean.

cathedral are very unimportant.

Britain is also the northern limit of the breeding range of the Dartford Warbler (described as a subspecies). Unfortunately these birds are declining quite rapidly and it is possible that they will be extinct in a decade or so. Destruction of many of the heaths on which they were formerly widespread, fires on the remaining heaths and, most important of all, severe winters have so reduced the British population that after each cold winter there are fewer and fewer of them about.

The Stone Curlew is another declining species, although in this case it was probably helped in the past by man's farming activities and so spread into areas in which it would have been otherwise unable to find suitable habitat. The arable areas are being slowly reduced by urban development, and one might expect their range to have become slightly more restricted; but they have in fact been decreasing rapidly, and no really satisfactory explanation has been found for this decline.

The birds of prey have probably suffered from man's activities more than any other group of birds – until very recently they were ruthlessly persecuted by gamekeepers, they are still shot in large numbers in many parts of southern Europe and, particularly since the 1950's, the mounting pollution resulting from the widespread use of agricultural pesticides has drastically reduced the populations of many species. Only recently has man really become aware of his responsibilities – but it may already be too late to bring the Peregrine back to most parts of its former range. On the brighter side there are the Ospreys which now breed successfully in Scotland every year (though nestlings ringed in protection-conscious Britain have been subsequently found shot in Spain).

One of the most seriously threatened group of habitats are the wetlands. Over the centuries more and more marshes, fens, swamps, bogs and saltings have been drained until only a handful survive. (Most of the artificial lakes and reservoirs created by man are too deep and not sufficiently overgrown to support an abundance of wildlife). The Rhone Delta and the Camargue in southern France, the Coto Donana in Spain, Neusiedl in Hungary and the Danube Delta in Romania are a few of the great wetlands which still survive – but most of these are threatened in some way. Up to 4,000 Flamingoes breed on the Camargue, one of the very few places they still exist in Europe, but in recent years they have been so disturbed by low flying aircraft that their breeding has been severely disrupted. The behaviour of the flamingo is such that every time they are frightened from the nest they go through an elaborate and extended ritual display when they return to incubate the eggs. The disturbance by aircraft has often been caused by tourists who want to see the spectacle of the flamingoes in flight – little do they realize that in so doing they are probably preventing the birds from breeding, but now a ban has been put on flights over the breeding grounds in an attempt to help the birds settle.

Above, the Grey Heron is the most common of the Herons in Britain and Europe, and is a shy and silent bird. They can frequently be seen standing motionless along the edge of coastal and inland waters watching for fish, or silently moving off to new grounds with languid flaps of their large wings.

Left, Curlews are one of the most attractive of the larger waders, and their beaks are so long that the birds seem to have three legs as they stump around the sands looking for worms and other invertibrates. Their silhouette in flight is distinctive because the short, wedge-shaped body seems almost too small to balance the curved beak. The Curlew's call is a loud and melancholy whistle, which often ends in a beautiful bubbling cadence.

Herons and bitterns are a group of birds almost entirely restricted to wetland habitats. Some of Europe's most beautiful birds are in this group and a mixed colony of herons is a magnificent sight. The most impressive species is undoubtedly the Great White Heron, or Large Egret as it is sometimes known. This splendid snowy-white bird was ruthlessly hunted at the turn of the century for its 'aigrettes' or 'ospreys' – the elegant plumes trailing from the back of the head – which had become fashionable hat decorations. It was around this bird that W H Hudson and the other founders of the bird protection movements fought one of the most successful of the early campaigns, and largely stopped the use of the plumes in millinery. The great white heron survived, but will it be able to survive the pressures on its habitat? The little egret, bittern, little bittern, squacco heron, grey heron,

purple heron, night heron, glossy ibis and spoonbill are all threatened to a greater or lesser extent. Almost everywhere their numbers are declining except where they are encouraged or protected, as the bittern is in East Anglia.

The Glossy Ibis is a species which was probably declining even without man's interference – but any further interference with the few remaining breeding colonies would be disastrous. Perhaps the saddest loss of all will be the pelicans. These huge birds which are so ungainly on land are one of the most majestic of all European birds when on the wing. The few remaining colonies in eastern Europe all seem doomed to extinction. At one time both the Dalmatian and the White Pelican were found on many of the larger wetlands, even in western Europe, but now the only sizeable breeding colonies are on the Danube Delta. Floods and fires in the reed beds in

Left, a Cattle Egret on its nest. This is one of the smallest of the Heron family and looks less ungainly in trees than some of its larger relatives. They take their name from their habit of feeding in fields round the feet, and sometimes actually on the backs, of cattle. They have recently crossed to North America and have spread very rapidly there.

Right, this Glossy Ibis belongs to a group of birds that is becoming increasingly rare all over the world. The Ibises are an ancient and handsome species, and are birds of the shores and marshes. The Glossy Ibis has very dark plumage which shines bronze and purple in the sun.

which they breed have taken their toll and tourist brochures still advertize the fact that pelicans can be shot by 'sportsmen', on payment of the appropriate fee.

In an area of marshland south of the Danube Delta ornithologists recently discovered vast flocks of wintering Red-breasted Geese. Previous to this there were no known wintering grounds of this species in Europe. Various other species of ducks and geese were also recorded in large numbers at this site, and elsewhere in Europe waterfowl are often being recorded in fantastic concentrations – a result of the de-

creasing number of suitable areas. Doubtless the Brent Geese which at present winter at Foulness will move away if London's third airport is built there, but where to?

An encouraging feature of waterfowl is that once attracted to a feeding ground they will often return to the same place year after year – at the Wildfowl Trust in Gloucester, the flock of Bewick's swans returns every year to the artificial lake and safety. If protected areas can be set up and, if necessary, extra food supplied, there is hope for the geese, swans and ducks – provided that the Arctic breeding grounds remain free

from interference and pollution.

The Great Bustard is one of the largest of European birds – in fact it is one of the heaviest flying birds in the world – and was at one time widespread over most of Europe and bred in Britain. Its extinction over most of its range is mainly due to hunting, though under strict protection it is slowly increasing in the eastern parts of its range. Both the great bustard and the little bustard have managed to adapt to cultivated areas and other man-made habitats (Madrid airport is one of the best places for seeing little bustard) and with protection there is no reason why they should not increase and eventually recolonize Britain.

In the cities the bird life is always changing, though few people are aware of the changes taking place. Some of the changes occur over a decade or so, while others take several centuries. In Medieval Europe ravens, jackdaws and black kites were common scavengers in cities. The Jackdaw manages to hang on in the parks of many cities in western Europe, but the other two have disappeared, except in a few parts of southern and eastern Europe. Their disappearance is largely due to changes in the methods of refuse disposal. The place of the ravens and kites is being taken by gulls, and the Herring Gull is often found nesting in seaside towns. Unfortunately the large increase in the numbers of these birds has probably caused the Audouin's Gull to decrease, as the larger gulls often kill and eat the chicks. Audouin's gull only breeds on a handful of islands in the Mediterranean area, and is one of the few species of bird that can be considered endemic to Europe.

Unlike a landmass such as Australia, Europe is not isolated from other regions of the world and consequently most European birds also occur outside Europe. The birds more or less restricted to Europe (some are also found in North Africa or parts of the Middle East) include Eleonora's Falcon, which breeds in the late summer in order to be able to feed its young on the migrant birds, and the Red-legged Partridge, a sedentary bird which has been successfully introduced into many places outside its native range. Two species of woodpecker are found mainly in Europe; the Green Woodpecker and the Great Spotted Woodpecker. A group of birds which often have rather re-

stricted ranges are the warblers. Several are restricted to Europe and North Africa including the Dartford warbler (mentioned earlier), Marmora's warbler, Subalpine warbler and Melodious warbler. The citril finch, serin and cirl bunting are also more or less confined to Europe.

Europe shares several species with North America – most of them are waders or sea birds but a few are passerines. The Wheatear, for instance, spread from Europe, probably via the British Isles, Iceland and Greenland to eastern North America. The birds from North America, Greenland and so on still return to Africa along the ancestral migration routes via Europe.

One species which has undoubtedly benefited in some way from man is the Collared Dove. This species was probably introduced into Europe from Asia Minor by the Turks. It remained a protected ornamental bird in towns in south-eastern Europe until the early part of this century when it began to spread its range. The expansion was mainly in a north-westerly direction and the first birds bred in England in 1955. They are now well established over most of Europe except the south-west and Italy. They are followers of human cultivation and also live in parks and gardens, but are rarely as common as the feral pigeons in the centre of towns.

The feral pigeons which are so abundant in the parks and squares in the centre of most large cities are the descendants of the domesticated rock doves which have reverted to a wild state. At one time they were an important source of meat during the winter months and were kept in huge dove cotes containing anything up to several thousand nests. By contrast with the feral pigeons, the Wood pigeon is normally shy and retiring, but in London and a few other places they have overcome their shyness and they now even breed in the centre of the metropolis.

When birds are not persecuted they often become remarkably tame. The Robin has been extensively hunted in the past and it is thought that this is one of the reasons why they are so shy – except in Britain, where they were fairly free from

persecution, and they are now extremely tame and confiding; so tame that they will often hop around a gardener's feet or perch on the fork while waiting for a worm to be exposed.

Other birds have become very tame, particularly members of the tit family. Most of them are hole nesting birds and readily take to nesting in man-made nest boxes. The last few years has seen bird-watching and bird protection move into the realm of big business and it is in the direction of garden birds that much of the effort is made. Suburban gardens are crammed with elaborate bird-tables, feeders dispensing well-known brands of bird food and a formidable array of nest-boxes to entice the birds to set up home. There is nothing like success to give encouragement and it is perhaps the tits who provide the encouragement to the bird 'gardener'. The tits are all active, highly acrobatic birds endowed with rather more intelligence than the average. They will even learn to perform simple tasks in order to obtain a food reward. Their ingenuity has led them to a habit which though amusing at first soon causes annoyance. They found that the contents of milk-bottles, left on door-steps, was tasty and have taken to pecking through the foil or cardboard cap to drink the best bit of the milk.

A wide variety of birds come to bird-tables to feed, some of them are just occasional visitors whilst others become as regular as the

Above, a large flock of Brent Geese spend the winter in the marshes near Foulness, and thus may be ousted by the new airport.

Below, a Bewick's Swan.

Pelicans are unfortunately becoming all too rare in Europe and are now only found on the Danube Delta. They are renowned for their antiquity, their enormous pouches, their sociability, and the rigid military regimentation of their lives. In flight they carry their heads well back with the heavy beaks resting partly on the folded neck.

great tits, blue tits, robins, house sparrows and starlings. The blackbirds, song thrushes and hedge sparrows rarely come to the table but they are a common enough sight elsewhere in the garden. In Britain the Great Spotted Woodpecker has become a regular visitor to garden bird-tables. Unfortunately they have a rather unpleasant habit of also visiting nest-boxes and enlarging the hole so that they can extract the young tits and eat them. This can be prevented by making a metal surround to the nest-box entrance.

Most hole nesting birds will readily take to artificial nesting-boxes. In Scandinavia nest-boxes used to be put up for goldeneye, smew and goosander in order to collect the down and the eggs, though nowadays the boxes are usually put up by conservationists. Other birds which often nest in artificial nest-boxes and nest-trays include starlings, wrynecks, pied wagtails, jackdaws, flycatchers, wheatears, redstarts, nuthatches, wrens and some of the owls.

Very often man has deliberately introduced birds into places in which they were unknown. Among the birds most commonly moved around in this way are the waterfowl. Ducks, geese and swans are popular both as hunter's quarry and also as ornamental fowl; a large number of species have been introduced into places outside their native range. One of the most successful introductions into Britain is the Canada Goose, which is now well established. In Sweden and other parts of Scandinavia it is even more successful and in winter migrates south to Germany and sometimes as far as the Netherlands or Switzerland. Over much of its range in Britain and Europe the Mute Swan has been introduced as an attractive addition to lakes and other waterways. The Grey-lag Goose from which the familiar farmyard goose is descended has been introduced or escaped into many parts of Europe – places from which man had at one time exterminated them. Many species of ducks are raised on ponds and lakes and after a few generations they too often go wild – the species involved are usually European in origin, but a few exotic species have also been

Above, this handsome Dalmation Pelican has a red-coloured gular pouch which will hold almost three gallons, though the bird uses it not as a larder but as a temporary dipnet for his catch.

Left, is one of the most exotic of all birds, the Mandarin Duck, which comes from eastern Asia and Japan and has been successfully introduced into Western Europe. This magnificent male shows off their dramatic colouring very well and notice in particular the striking orange 'sails' which curve over his back.

Left, the intelligent and determined little Blue Tit is a favourite in practically every garden. Pert and friendly, their acrobatic feeding habits are most entertaining to watch and they are very satisfactory visitors to nesting boxes of virtually any type and shape.

Right, the male Great Bustard has a marvellous display and transforms himself into a great fluffy white bird as he turns his feathers inside out and struts in front of the female.

Below, a pair of handsome Goldfinches – these birds are among the most attractive of the regular visitors to large gardens. The flash of gold and crimson is unmistakable as they flit from tree to tree in pairs or small groups, and they also have a beautiful song.

introduced. The most successful of the exotics in Britain is the Mandarin Duck, which originally came from the Far East. This bizarre looking duck is mainly found in well wooded areas where it nests in trees. Other waterfowl successfully introduced into Britain include the Egyptian Goose and the American Ruddy Duck.

Game birds have also frequently been the subjects for attempts at introduction. One of the first introductions was undoubtedly the pheasant which is now widespread not only in Britain and Europe but also in North America, New Zealand and elsewhere. In recent years other pheasants have been released in Britain and some, such as the Golden Pheasant and Lady Amherst's Pheasant are still holding their own. The Red-legged Partridge is well established in many places outside its original range – in many parts of Britain it is now commoner than the native partridge. The Capercaillies now found in Scotland were in fact introduced. The native birds, which were once widespread, died out mainly due to over shooting and the present Scottish population are descendants of birds introduced from Sweden in 1837.

The Little Owl was brought to Britain in the nineteenth century and is one of the most successful of the introduced birds, as it has established itself over a wide area without drastically altering the natural balance, as have so many other introductions. Many people have attempted to establish storks in various parts of Europe, including Britain, but none have met with

much success even when reintroducing them into places they once inhabited. The main reason for this failure is probably the disappearance of suitable habitat.

The coasts of Europe are often good places to search for waders. Holland has always attracted a good deal of attention from bird-watchers though there are many other areas equally good – perhaps it is just that Holland is a more convenient place to watch them. Sometimes the numbers are vast – it is estimated that nearly 200,000 oystercatchers and over 25,000 curlew together with 20,000 or more bar-tailed godwit, up to 80,000 dunlin and over 50,000 knot may winter in the Waddenzee area of Holland. In summer and on passage a wide variety of other waders can also be seen. The avocets in Holland are a magnificent sight, and it is presumably the overspill from the Dutch breeding colonies which colonized England.

The avocets are now well established at Minsmere and a few other localities in East Anglia, but a more recent arrival is the Ruff which, although a common passage migrant, had not nested regularly in England for nearly 80 years – it still remains to be seen whether or not it manages to recolonize England. Many of the waders nest well away from water and most of the birds seen in such profusion along the coasts will have bred far away, possibly in Lapland or even Siberia.

Some species of birds are irruptive – that is to say that periodically they perform large migrations and appear in places well outside their normal range. Sometimes this occurs every few years but in some species it only occurs at very irregular

Top, the Collared Turtle Dove is a tame and attractive bird with a characteristic, deep-chested, three note cooing.

Left, a Robin's song is one of the most distinctive and musical to be heard regularly in the garden – usually the bird is claiming his territory and calling to a mate.

Right, a Great Spotted Woodpecker about to enter its nest hole. It is a striking black and white bird with red splashes on neck and undertail feathers.

intervals. The Pallas's Sand Grouse is normally only found in the steppes of central Asia but on occasions it has spread right across into western Europe as far as Britain and has even settled down to nest. The cause of the irruptions is not fully understood, but in many species it is certainly connected with the food supply. Species such as the Nutcracker and the Waxwing invade western Europe every few years when the food supply in their native Scandinavia fails. Other species appear in large numbers after particularly successful breeding seasons – the Short-eared Owl feeds extensively on the short-tailed vole, a small mammal which builds up to 'plague' proportions similar to those of the better known lemmings; when the voles are abundant the short-eared owls enjoy a very successful breeding season and will often appear in unexpected places subsequently. Most of the irruptive species return to their former range to breed, but some species colonize new areas. Crossbills periodically invade the British Isles from northern Europe and some usually remain and breed for several years afterwards if conditions are suitable.

Many of the birds breeding in Europe are migratory. Some spend just a few months in Europe and then migrate south to spend the winter in Africa, while others merely move from the northern parts of Europe to the south and west. In order to study bird migration observatories have been established in many parts of Europe. The observatories are usually situated on islands or headlands where the migrating birds tend to concentrate. Each year bird-watchers gather at Falsterbo in southern Sweden in order to watch the bird of prey migration; and the Bosphorus is remarkable for the vast numbers of storks and birds of prey which gather there in the autumn; Heligoland, Fair Isle, the Isles of Scilly, Capri and Bardsey are just a few of the islands which have bird observatories on them. Bird-watchers at these places see not only large numbers of common migrants but also stragglers and rarities, often hundreds of miles off course. On St Agnes in the Isles of Scilly, for instance, unusual

Canada Geese are the most widespread and well known of the geese in North America and have been very successfully introduced in Britain where they are frequently seen on farm ponds and lakes. Their black necks and heads with white cheeks are unmistakable.

migrants from north and east Europe have included red-breasted fly-catcher, greenish warbler, arctic warbler, eye-browed thrush, rustic bunting and bluethroat; birds from southern Europe which have wandered off course include subalpine warbler, melodious warbler, ortolan bunting, woodchat, shrike, hoopoe and alpine swift; birds which have come from North America include buff-breasted sandpiper, pectoral sandpiper, white-rumped sandpiper and least sandpiper, and – even more surprising than the above waders – several passerine species

including bobolink, northern water thrush, red-eyed vireo and American robin. These passerine species normally get to Europe by travelling part of the way on board ships, where they pick up scraps of food on the deck, and leave as soon as land is in sight – hence their regular occurrence on Scilly, way out in the Atlantic.

What does the future hold for the birds of Europe? This is of course the 64,000 dollar question that every ornithologist would like to be able to answer. Undoubtedly there is much that is depressing – the human

population is expanding at an alarming rate and as it does so the countryside is 'developed'. On the brighter side there is also a more enlightened approach and at last the biologists are being listened to. Some species of birds may only be able to survive in reserves – ibises, many of the herons, pelicans, geese and swans may not be able to exist unless land is put aside expressly for them. Others, as we have seen, are capable of adapting to the artificial habitats created by man – some of the gulls, the bustards, martins, swallows, swifts, sparrows, pigeons and starl-ings have all managed in some way to benefit from man's activities. The great majority of birds, however, coexist with man rather precariously and if the balance is tilted much more against the birds the future will not be very bright. Parks, gardens, commons, heaths, lakes, rivers and so on all need to be conserved carefully to ensure that there will be wild birds for future generations to enjoy. Birds cannot be protected or conserved in a vacuum – it is important that the whole environment is properly managed.

An Avocet at its nest. These are very handsome black and white wading birds with extremely long legs and a delicate, black, upturned bill. They prefer sheltered bays and lakes and feed in large flocks, calling to each other with soft, musical twitterings all the time.

Birds of North America

WHITNEY AND KAREN EASTMAN

The area covered in this chapter is the area covered by the American Ornithologists' Union and includes the lower forty-eight states of the United States, plus Alaska, all of the Dominion of Canada, the islands of Bermuda and Greenland and Baja California, Mexico. This is a vast area with almost every variety of habitat, including three ocean shores, several large mountain ranges, several large river systems such as the Mississippi; thousands of lakes (the State of Minnesota is known as the Land of 10,000 Lakes), extensive prairie and grazing lands and cultivated farm land; the deserts of Arizona and California, the tropical area of southern Florida and the semi-tropical areas of Texas, Arizona and California; and finally the vast tundra of Alaska and Canada. Thus it is evident that many different birds of all kinds are represented in North America. There are three main north–south migration flyways, the Pacific flyway, the Mississippi flyway and the Atlantic flyway, with several intermediate routes.

The A.O.U. Check-List of 1957 lists 1,683 species and sub-species (geographic races), and there are approximately 800 full species in seventy-five families which may be observed in the area. This number is constantly changing as birds become extinct or different species from other areas settle in new territory, or new species are introduced and become established. While the largest number of species may be observed during the spring, summer and fall months, some of our migrants linger with us in winter, increasing the number of species to be seen in the South. For many years the National Audubon Society in collaboration with the U.S. Fish and Wildlife Service has taken a Christmas Bird Count, and the seventy-first Christmas Bird Count taken in December 1970 by 16,657 observers, reported altogether 561 species.

Since the number of species is too large to include in a single chapter and do justice to each, certain typical species have been selected from the seventy-five families for individual treatment.

While we have four species of loons in North America, the Common Loon (*Gavia immer*) is by far the best known and is seen and enjoyed by a great many people. This species nests all across the northern latitudes from the Atlantic to the Pacific; and in particular on the shores and islands of many of the 10,000 lakes in Minnesota, where it is the official state bird. The nest is built close to the water as loons cannot navigate well on land, and two eggs is the usual clutch. The voice is a beautiful rhapsody, and the evening song is much appreciated by those who are so fortunate as to live or camp nearby. The sound recording, *A Day in Algonquin Park*,

A Western Grebe carrying its chick under its wing feathers – a habit common to all Grebes.

24

published by the Federation of
Ontario Naturalists, gives a complete repertoire. They winter on
salt water in the southern part of
the United States.

Of the six species of grebes in
North America, the Western Grebe
(*Aechmophorus occidentalis*) is considered by many observers to be the
most beautiful and graceful. As its
name implies, the nesting and wintering range is in western North
America from Manitoba and Minnesota (rarely) west to the Pacific
Coast. They winter south of the

nesting range, abundantly on the
Pacific Coast, and only rarely in the
southern states.

This bird is easily identified as it
sits low on the water by its extra-
ordinarily long white neck, long
pointed bill and dark back. The
most beautiful avian nuptial exhibi-
tion we have been privileged to
observe was performed by the Western Grebe, and took place on a lake
in western Minnesota. The birds
rise up on their tiptoes, and with
wings flapping furiously and with
their long sharp bills pointed for-

ward, run swiftly back and forth across the water. The performance resembles a beautiful ballet which centuries of practice has made perfect.

There are two pelicans in North America, the Brown Pelican and the White Pelican, and the former (*Pelecanus occidentalis*) is one of the species that is in danger of dying out. At one time it was a common breeder along the Atlantic, Pacific and Gulf coasts, but because of the presence of large amounts of DDT found in the surface fish on which

they feed, they are now producing soft-shelled eggs. Very few nests on the California coast produce any young. It is the state bird of Louisiana, though it is now a rarity on the Gulf coast of this state; in Florida there are still a few successful nesting colonies, but the reproduction rate is declining fast. However, when we were in the Galapagos Islands in 1970, it was heartening to see large numbers of Brown Pelicans, and perhaps the Galapagos will be their last stand.

The Anhinga (*Anhinga anhinga*),

known commonly by its scientific name (as very few birds are), is the only species in its family in North America. It is a strange bird – comical to watch. It is a marvellous swimmer under water searching for fish, but appears to hang itself out to dry frequently with wings outspread. It is often called the snakebird as it swims with its long snake-like neck sticking up above the surface. The plumage and habits of this species are unusual since the female sports the more colourful attire, while the male performs a large

The Anhingas are very closely allied to the Cormorant family and inhabit the wooded banks of freshwater lakes, swamps and rivers.

which they forage for food over large areas extending miles from their nesting sites.

The Wood Ibis or Wood Stork (*Mycteria americana*), our only North American stork, has captured the interest of the conservationists, since there has been great concern that this species might suffer a severe decline in numbers and protective measures have been taken in recent years to rebuild the population. The centre of population is along the Gulf Coast from Texas to Florida, though it may be also observed along the south-west Pacific Coast. With the continued drainage and pollution of their fresh water feeding areas along the coastal belt, some years pass when Wood Storks do not nest at all because of lack of food supplies sufficient to feed themselves and their young.

The National Audubon Society has assumed the leading role in providing suitable habitat for this species. The Society owns and operates Corkscrew Swamp Sanctuary in south-western Florida. Its 11,000 acres contain the largest remaining stand of virgin bald cypress, the oldest trees in eastern North America, which provide nesting sites for the Wood Storks. In 1971 over two thousand nests produced young. Because of drainage in the surrounding crop land the birds had to fly great distances to find food, so to insure a food supply for both parents and young the Audubon Society has now built extensive food rearing ponds on old tomato fields and stocked them with various kinds of fish and marine life under controlled water levels within the sanctuary area. Thus man has restored in this instance what man has destroyed.

The Roseate Spoonbill (*Ajaia ajaja*) is one of our most beautiful birds and is a thrilling sight. It is pink, scarlet and white and has a long spatulate bill with a spoon-like device at the tip. This is elaborately equipped with a straining mechanism to permit the bird to separate its food from extraneous material while swinging its bill back and forth sidewise in the soft marl in shallow water. It is found along the Gulf Coast from Texas to Florida, and the largest breeding

share of the domestic chores. It is common in suitable swampy habitat along the Gulf Coast, particularly in Florida, as well as inland points such as Wakulla Springs.

Of the thirteen herons and egrets found in North America, the Great Blue Heron (*Ardea herodias*) is the best known by the 'rank and file' bird-watcher. It is a stately bird, about four feet tall, and when adorned in its nuptial plumage, is a beautiful creature, or even when just standing erect or slowly stalking its prey, it is a thing of striking grace. Great Blues migrate north from their southern wintering range in early spring as soon as the ice leaves the lakes and streams, and spend the summer in rookeries from

colony is in the Florida Keys. Within the sanctuaries established by National Audubon along the coast, they are making a good comeback after being decimated by the plume hunters. After their breeding season is over in early spring, many birds make a limited post-nuptial flight northward, and as many as 200 birds come to Sanibel Island, Florida, to feed and spend the spring and summer months in the Ding Darling Sanctuary. They are one of the main attractions for the winter visitors to this lovely island, world-famous for its sea shells as well as its birds.

The Trumpeter Swan (*Olor buccinator*), the largest of the four swans occurring in North America was close to extinction forty years ago, but through the heroic efforts of the U.S. Bureau of Sports Fisheries and Wildlife and dedicated groups of conservationists in the U.S. and Canada we now have 4,000 to 5,000 of these stately birds under protection, according to recent surveys. The bulk of this species resides in Yellowstone Park in Wyoming, Red Rock Lakes National Wildlife Refuge in Montana, Alaska and the Canadian Rockies. However, conservationists have transferred cygnets from Red Rock Lakes and established them in several refuges in the United States and Canada where they formerly bred. In Carver Park Refuge, thirty miles from Minneapolis, we had the first pair nest

The Great Blue Heron is the largest of the Heron family and is an imposing and beautiful bird which is well-known in North America.

in Minnesota since 1880, and we now have a free-flying flock of Trumpeters of about twenty birds.

The Wood Duck (*Aix sponsa*) is considered by many to be the most handsome bird in America, although several other species also claim this distinction. They have a wide nesting range all across Canada and the United States, and though some winter south of the U.S. border, the majority winters in the Gulf states. Hunting pressure reduced this species to a dangerous level, but when the number of Wood Ducks in the hunter's daily bag was limited to one during the hunting season their numbers started to increase again. Another factor which has encouraged this comeback has been the large number of Wood Duck houses erected in recent years to take the place of nesting holes in trees, the usual nesting site for this duck. An interesting sidelight is the fact that the female selects her mate on their wintering grounds, and then leads her new mate back to her ancestral home to nest. Thus a male Wood Duck may nest in New England one year and in Minnesota the next.

The Bald Eagle (*Haliaeetus leucocephalus*), the National Emblem of the United States of America, is a majestic bird, admired for its beauty and grace in flight. It flies with deep wing strokes and soars on flat wings. It reaches maturity during the fourth year when the birds acquire their white heads and white tails, though the rest of the body at maturity remains brown. The range is along rivers and lakes from the Gulf of Mexico to the Arctic and they winter as far north as open water exists and they are able to find fish for food. Their principal food is surface fish which in recent years have built up large quantities of DDT in the fatty tissues, causing the Bald Eagle to lay infertile eggs with soft shells. This means that the population in the lower forty-eight states of the United States and Canada has declined rapidly, though there is still a sizeable population in Alaska. Before Alaska became the fiftieth state of the United States and the Bald Eagle was placed on the protected list, the salmon fishermen took a heavy toll of these birds, claiming that they were reducing the salmon supply. Even now the numbers continue to fall, and another reason may be poison – quite recently a large number of Bald Eagles along with some Golden Eagles were found poisoned in Wyoming after eating the dead carcasses put out by ranchers and predator control groups to kill coyotes. The National Audubon Society carries out a Bald Eagle survey each year and has stated that the population is seriously threatened.

There are three species of ptarmigan in North America – the Willow (*Lagopus lagopus*), the Rock (*Lagopus mutus*) and the White-tailed (*Lagopus leucurus*). They are all birds of the snow country, and they all have one thing in common; they are well camouflaged all the year round being brown during the breeding season and turning white in winter. One might expect to find these birds only in high country, but such is not always the case, since we have seen both the Willow Ptarmigan and the Rock Ptarmigan near sea level.

The Whooping Crane (*Grus americana*), one of the rarest and most esteemed species in America, is making a slow recovery after reaching a low population of wild birds in 1941–42 of thirteen adults and two young. The wild bird flock nests in remote muskeg in Wood Buffalo Park in northern Canada

Two birds that have been 'rescued' from declining rapidly in numbers are Wood Storks and Trumpeter Swans. The natural habitat of the Wood Storks (above) was fast disappearing until the Anderson Society established a sanctuary in southwest Florida. The Trumpeter Swan (left) is the largest of all the Swans and is a striking and impressive bird which was severely hunted for its meat. It can now be seen in several of the National Parks.

and winters in Aransas National Wildlife Refuge near Austwell, Texas. This means that their migration route covers nearly 2,600 miles. The wild flock on wintering grounds in 1970 numbered fifty seven – fifty one adults and six young – a gain of one bird over the previous year, but the highest number since the low point in 1941–42. The food supply of the wild flock on their wintering grounds, consisting of blue crabs, shrimp, frogs and worms, has been endangered in recent years by dredging operations adjacent to the refuge. Since there is no other wintering site available anywhere in the South, the wild flock is still in danger.

In 1945 the National Audubon Society and the U.S. Fish and Wildlife Service established a co-operative Whooping Crane Project; the joint effort to save this regal species was later joined by the Canadian government and was responsible for discovering the nesting grounds in Canada. To augment the wild flock, one egg has been removed from each of several nests in Canada and flown to the Patuxent Wildlife Research Refuge at Laurel, Maryland, where they have been hatched in incubators. It is planned to release captive birds to the wild flock at some future date.

The Limpkin (*Aramus guarauna*), known as the crying bird, is the only species in its family, and is found locally in Florida. They are rather tame and can be studied at close range; one place where an observer is sure of seeing the bird is at Wakulla Springs near Tallahassee in northern Florida. Limpkins live almost entirely on snails, and the long, slender, slightly decurved bill is well adapted for

extracting the snails from their shells. Their cry is a bloodcurdling sound which is heard mostly at night, especially during the breeding season.

There are a large number of interesting shore birds in North America, which provide great excitement for field observers. Some of these are rarities such as the Eskimo Curlew, which may be extinct, since the last time this species was observed was in Texas on migration several years ago. The European Ruff visits us occasionally, and one of these rare vagrants spent several days in Minnesota in the spring of 1971. The male bird all dressed up in beautiful black-phase nuptial plumage attracted large groups of observers.

The Ruddy Turnstone (*Arenaria interpres*) has short orange-red legs and in flight presents a beautiful pattern of black, reddish-brown and white. They feed in large flocks on the beaches of Florida, and have the habit of turning over small stones, sea shells and seaweed in search of food – hence the name. At Churchill on Hudson Bay, Canada, in June 1970, we observed huge flocks of them en route to their nesting grounds in the Arctic, and in August 1967 we visited the Pribilof Islands and observed tremendous numbers in migration from their nesting grounds in the Arctic – they formed a moving carpet feeding on the upland grasslands.

One of the most unusual birds we have in North America is the Roadrunner (*Geococcyx californianus*). It is a bird of the desert in the south-western part of the United States, and belongs to the family of cuckoos – it is often called the ground cuckoo. Some say it can outrun a horse, and it seldom takes to the air. It has a large distinctive crest and a long white-tipped tail,

Left, the Wood Duck is one of the most colourful and boldly marked of all the birds of North America, and is very similar to the Mandarin Duck which has been introduced successfully in Europe.

Below, the Roadrunner is a very unusual bird which lives in the desert feeding on snakes and lizards, and rarely takes to the air at all.

and is greatly admired by most residents in its area, as it feeds very largely on snakes, lizards and insects. In some desert areas it is quite common, but because it skulks and keeps to the ground relatively few people ever get a glimpse of it.

The family of hummingbirds is confined to the New World. The A.O.U. Check-List lists nineteen species for North America. Only one of these, the Ruby-throated Hummingbird (*Archilochus colubris*), occurs regularly in the eastern part of our area. The male Ruby-throat is a handsome sprite with a sparkling green back, white belly

and a flaming red gorget. To see the gorgets of hummingbirds well one needs a good binocular and must have good light with the sun behind the observer, for the colour is dependent upon light refraction. Their nest is a work of art, adorned and camouflaged with lichen and spider webs, and the clutch comprises two eggs about the size of peas. The tiny Ruby-throat's feat in crossing the Gulf of Mexico in migration is a source of wonder to ornithologists.

The North American family of woodpeckers numbers twenty two species, some of which may be found

throughout the entire area. In this group we have two very large species – the Pileated Woodpecker and the Ivory-billed Woodpecker (*Campephilus principalis*), which is the largest and is close to extinction. It was thought to be extinct about twenty years ago, but we rediscovered a pair in the Chipola River swamp near Blountstown, Florida on March 3, 1950, and established a sanctuary under the auspices of the National Audubon Society. The pair remained in the sanctuary area for nearly three years but unfortunately did not produce young. We are still having sightings reported from Texas, South Carolina and Florida,

so it is presumed that there is still a small remnant. However, because of the destruction of the large trees which provide their food in the swamps of the South where this species has lived since before Audubon's time, this great bird appears to be doomed.

The other large species, the Pileated Woodpecker (*Dryocopus pileatus*), slightly smaller than the Ivory-bill, was at a low ebb around the turn of the century but is making a strong recovery. It has an extensive range all across Canada and the United States to the Gulf of Mexico. On the island of Sanibel off the south-west coast of Florida it is not

Above, the Phoebe Flycatcher is one of the smaller of the numerous family of New World Flycatchers, and is typically olive brown and buff in colour. It has a distinctive and incessant song which it keeps up all day from its perch, only stopping to dart out in pursuit of flies.

Right, a female Ruby-throated Hummingbird hovers with rapid wing beats while feeding the young bird, which is almost too big for the tiny nest. The females do not have the jewel-like colours of the males and build the intricate nest and rear the young alone.

Left, two Pileated Woodpeckers, very handsome birds which can be seen most easily on the island of Sanibel, as they are not as common as they used to be, and are rather shy. Like all Woodpeckers they work hard for their living, probing tree trunks searching for grubs and larvae, and are in consequence solitary birds.

Right, Blue Jays are a common sight in North America and have a prominent light blue crest which they raise whenever excited or angry.

Below, the Limpkin got its name from its halting, limping gait, and is also known as the 'Crying Bird' after its loud and mournful cry.

unusual in driving the length of the island to see a half dozen of them on telephone poles and trees along the roadway. It is a spectacular bird to watch. Both sexes have large scarlet crests with black and white cheeks, prominent white stripes down the neck and an all black body when perched. The male has a scarlet moustache. In flight large white windows appear in the wings.

The family of flycatchers comprises a large number of species, widely distributed over much of our area, which vary greatly in size and colouration. They feed on insects, and usually leave their perch for a second to dart out and catch them mid-air. Of this family the Great Crested Flycatcher (*Myiarchus crinitus*) is one of the larger species and is a strikingly handsome bird with a broad bill, large head with a prominent crest, lemon yellow belly and a long, rusty tail. They nest in

tree cavities, woodpecker holes and nest boxes, differing from the rest of the flycatcher family, and have an inherited habit of placing a cast snakeskin in their nesting cavity, presumably for predator protection. When the birds do not find a snakeskin handy, they substitute a piece of cellophane.

The Blue Jay (*Cyanocitta cristata*) is one of the commonest and best known birds in eastern North America, breeding all the way from central Canada to Florida. It is a beautiful bird with its prominent light blue crest and black collar separating its white face from the light blue back and tail. It is the only blue-coloured jay with white blotches in the wings and white tail feathers. Most observers feel that this species is a 'robber' because it is charged with stealing eggs and young from other birds' nests and often monopolizes feeding stations. A bird

of the forest, it often nests near homes and furnishes amusement for bird-watchers.

The Black-capped Chickadee (*Parus atricapillus*) is a bird of the hardwood forest, and many birds remain in their breeding area all winter. It is a friendly, confiding bird, providing companionship all the year round for the woodsman and for many home owners who provide suitable food – suet and sunflower seed – to attract them. Chickadees nest in one of our wren houses in our yard in Minneapolis and last year (1970) brought off a brood of seven, this year a brood of eight.

The House Wren (*Troglodytes aedon*) brings much pleasure to those whom they honour by occupying a nesting box or other suitable location near their homes. Some years ago during their northern migration the population was greatly

Above, the Mockingbird is the 'State Bird' of five of the Southern States, and is noted for its singing and powers of mimicry.

Below, Cedar Waxwings looking for berries.

Right, the House Wren is even better known in America than the Winter or Jenny 'Wren', probably because it is not fussy as to where it builds its nest and is a most regular user of nesting boxes. Like all Wrens they have loud and beautiful voices.

Top, the Cardinal is a fiery red bird with a black face and throat patch, which lives in eastern North America.

Above, a Prothonotory Warbler, one of America's brightest golden yellow birds. A flight of these Warblers in breeding plumage passing through a field in spring is a wonderful sight.

Top right, the busy little Blue-grey Gnatcatcher which is found throughout America.

Opposite, this Black-capped Chickadee is one of the Tit family and has all the attractive characteristics of the group.

reduced by a bad snowstorm, but they have since made a strong comeback. This species is very friendly to man but is an aggressive fighter if any bird, even many times its size, comes near its nest. If nesting boxes are not available, they will nest in your mailbox, a clothes-pin bag, the pocket of an old coat or a crevice in your house or barn. Audubon depicted them nesting in an old hat.

This species is often polygynous, the male having as many as three females in his harem. He comes north in advance and selects nest sites and stakes out his territory. Then he sings his heart out to attract females as they arrive in the area. Each female normally brings off two broods each year.

The Mockingbird (*Mimus poly-glottos*) is one of our most melodious songsters, and often sings at night, especially on moonlight nights. It repeats most phrases of its song many times. and is also a 'pro-fessional' mimic able to fool many people as to its identity if it is hidden. While the Mockingbird is generally considered a bird of the Deep South, in recent years it has been expanding its range as far north as Canada.

The American Robin (*Turdus migratorius*) is quite different from the European Robin, and is without doubt the best known and loved of any member of the thrush family. It has a wide nesting distribution all across North America, and usually winters in the Gulf states. When they come north in early spring, they follow the frost line as they feed almost entirely on earthworms at this time of year. Later they become *fruit* eaters, indulging in all kinds of fruit available, as they do in winter in the South – the berries of the Brazilian pepper tree and of the cabbage palm being particularly popular. In winter in Florida we have observed huge flocks, number-ing into the thousands, come into an

Above, the American Robin is like a European Thrush with a red breast, and is a friendly and attractive bird with a beautiful song.

Right, a male Red-winged Blackbird. These are principally marsh birds and are very gregarious, breeding and migrating in vast flocks.

area, staying only until they have exhausted the food supply and then moving on.

The Robin is a beautiful songster, particularly at daybreak and twilight. They are also relatively tame, confiding birds, nesting close to our homes and returning year after year to the same place to breed.

The Blue-grey Gnatcatcher (*Polioptila caerulea*) is a lively little sprite, always on the move. It is a beautiful bird with a blue-grey back, prominent eye-ring and a fairly long tail, bordered with white feathers on both sides, and it looks like a miniature Mockingbird. It has a habit of twitching the tail sideways, and the voice is a fairly high nasal call. They nest all the way north to southern Canada from the Atlantic to the Pacific. Some winter in our southern states, especially Florida, but most winter south of the United States. Taking a Christmas bird count in Mexico several years ago, we found it almost impossible to

record their number with any degree of accuracy, so ubiquitous was the little call of 'spee' on all sides.

On their winter range in Florida where we have observed this species for many years, they are very tame and confiding. They always appear to be in a happy mood while at work and pay little attention to an observer or photographer a few feet away, but trying to catch them still for an instant is most frustrating.

The Cedar Waxwing (*Bombycilla cedrorum*) appears to be our best groomed bird. They always look as though they have just come from the beauty parlour – never a feather out of place. They give the impression that they are very polite, and we have observed a long line of these birds perched on a wire, passing a cherry back and forth several times until some famished bird dared to swallow it.

They are easily identified by their long distinctive yellowish brown crests, black face masks, yellowish

brown backs, dark wings, yellow bellies, yellow-tipped tails and a red wax-like spot at the tips of the secondaries. Sexes are alike. They feed largely on fruit, showing a preference for berries and cherries.

Their breeding and wintering ranges are not well defined, but they nest from as far north as Alaska down to south of our border and winter mostly in the southern United States where fruit is available. They are seldom seen alone except during the breeding season, after which they gather in large flocks and move about gypsy-like in their wintering range in search of food to their liking.

There are about fifty warblers to be observed in our area, all of which are very popular and eagerly sought after by bird-watchers, particularly when they are in breeding plumage during migration north in spring. We have selected as our favourite the Prothonotory Warbler (*Protonotaria citrea*). This is a strikingly

beautiful bird with its golden head, golden-yellow underparts and blue-grey wings. Their usual habitat is swamps and tree-lined streams where they nest in holes in trees or old stumps. They will occupy man-made nesting boxes if available in their breeding habitat. Some years ago we observed a small colony of these birds nesting in coffee cans with a man-made nest hole, placed along the shore of a lake in Wisconsin. In this hereditary habit of nest site selection they differ from the rest of the members of the Parulidae group. They nest from the Gulf of Mexico north as far as

Maine and Minnesota and winter south of our border to South America.

The most numerous species in the family Icteridae is the Red-winged Blackbird (*Agelaius phoeniceus*). This species breeds from Canada to the Gulf of Mexico and winters largely in the southern part of the United States, though there are several races which are resident in the Gulf states. The male is all black with the exception of its brilliant red shoulder patch, bordered on the lower part by a yellow band. The female is a brownish, nondescript, streaked bird with at times a semblance of the

Above, Turnstones preening on a cliff edge.

Right, the Willow Grouse or Ptarmigan goes completely white in winter so that it is perfectly camouflaged in the snow.

male's shoulder patch. After nesting they gather in huge flocks for the winter months in the South. They are considered to be very destructive to farmers' crops although their insectivorous habits most of the year are beneficial. The 1970 National Audubon Christmas Bird Count report lists the largest concentration of this species as 6,400,000 birds at Little Rock, Arkansas. The population has increased enormously as modern agricultural methods have favoured them. They are expanding from the marshes into previously unexploited habitat.

Probably the best known of the nine orioles to be observed in our area is the Baltimore Oriole (*Icterus galbula*). This is a species of the eastern United States and Canada, replaced in the West by Bullock's Oriole. It breeds from Canada to the Gulf and winters below our border except for a few that linger here and there all winter. The male is a beautiful creature with his contrasting black head, brilliant orange underparts and lower back, black wings with prominent white wing bars and orange and black tail. The Orioles' hanging, pendulous nest is a work of art. Their principal foods are insects, fruit and nectar from flowers. While we are writing this chapter, we have several pairs and young feeding at our patio feeders where we supply oranges (cut in half), grape jelly and red-coloured sugar water (20% white sugar).

The Cardinal (*Richmondena cardinalis*), known as the Red Bird locally in the South, is familiar throughout its range. It derived its name because its plumage resembles the tight-fitting red cassock worn by a cardinal of the clergy. The male is garbed in fiery red plumage with a large red erect crest and black face and throat patch. The female is beautiful, too, in a more subdued way – brownish with touches of red. It is a resident of eastern North America, and in recent years has extended its range northwards into Canada. In the North especially they patronize feeding stations on a year around basis where their favourite food is sunflower seed. Originally a bird of the South, this habit has undoubtedly encouraged

the extension of its range. The Cardinal's song is a loud repetitive whistle and they sing in every month of the year here in Minnesota even on the coldest days in winter.

The Rose-breasted Grosbeak (*Pheucticus ludovicianus*) is a friendly and confiding bird. It breeds in eastern United States from Canada as far south as Georgia, and has been observed as far west as California in migration. It winters south of our border to South America, and is replaced in the West by the Black-headed Grosbeak. The male Rose-breasted is a handsome creature, with its rose-coloured breast,

black head and back with prominent white wing bars. In flight the beautiful rose-coloured wing linings show. The female is a heavily streaked brownish bird with the typical grosbeak bill. Several pairs nest in our woods at our home in Minneapolis and patronize our feeding stations all summer long. Their favourite food at feeding stations is sunflower seed, and the amount they consume is enormous.

The Painted Bunting (*Passerina ciris*) is considered by many observers to be the most beautiful bird in North America. Locally in certain areas it is known as

Nonpareil. This species breeds from the Gulf states (Texas to Florida) north to southern Missouri and North Carolina. Most winter south of our border, but many remain with us all winter in the Gulf states – especially in Florida. Their food consists largely of weed seeds, but when attracted to feeding stations in the South in winter, they are very fond of the small hard seed usually fed to caged birds. The adult male is a riot of brilliant colours with head and nape dark violet-blue, back yellow-green, wings and tail black and rump and underparts scarlet.

The sober female has the upper parts green and the underparts yellowish-green.

Authors' note: for field identification purposes, we recommend the following pocket field guides:
Roger Tory Peterson – *A Field Guide to the Birds* – Eastern North America.
Roger Tory Peterson – *A Field Guide to Western Birds.*
Robbins, Bruun, Zim – *Birds of North America* – A Guide to Field Identification for both eastern and western species.

Above, a beautiful photograph showing the striking and complex plumage of the Black-throated Diver. The head and back of the neck are pale grey in colour, and the feathers are very soft and dense.

Right, the Eurasian Spoonbill is very similar to the Roseate Spoonbill except that it does not have the beautiful pink plumage of its New World relative.

Above, a male Baltimore Oriel
arrives in the eastern United States
and Canada in spring parading his
lovely orange and black colours. The
Oriels are among the best songsters
and the best architects of the bird
world, though it is the drab coloured
female which weaves the intricate
hanging nest while the male spends
his time chasing insects and singing.

Above right, the male Painted
Bunting is often considered to be the
most beautiful bird to breed in North
America, but he is not often seen.

Right, a young Turquoise-browed
Motmot sits quietly on a branch in
the forest flicking its tail from side to
side – they do this for long periods
and their placid demeanour has led
the Spaniards to call them 'bobo' or
fool. As the bird grows and preens
itself the two central tail feathers will
lose their vanes except at the end so
that they are racquet tipped.

Above, a few of the beautiful Lesser Flamingoes that throng the Rift Valley Lakes of East Africa in hundreds of thousands and are a major tourist attraction. They have the longest legs and necks in proportion to their bodies of any bird in the world, and when flying both are stretched out quite straight.

Right, a regal Sunbird, looking rather pugnacious. These birds are considered the counterparts of the New World Hummingbirds and rival them in brilliance and variety of colour, though not in flying prowess. There are 104 species, all tiny, and they have particularly long tongues with forked tips for feeding on the nectar they find in flowers.

Exotic and colourful birds

MALCOLM ELLIS

Central and South America

Nowhere is there a greater number and diversity of species of birds than in Central and South America. It is the home of many of the 300 or more species of tiny jewel-like hummingbirds, jacamars, puffbirds, the toucans with their gaily coloured bills, and a multitude of gaudy-plumaged parrots, macaws, and other exotic species. The screamers, Hoatzin (*Opisthocomus hoazin*), *Sunbitten* (*Eurypyga helias*), and the unique, nocturnal, fruit-eating Oilbird (*Steatornis caripensis*), are among the birds indigenous to the region, which in zoological terms stretches south from the tropical rain forest of Mexico to Cape Horn, and includes the West Indies.

With their brilliant irridescent feathering, embracing almost every conceivable colour, the tiny hummingbirds can surely be called nature's living jewels. Their plumage, rich in greens, blues, purples and reds, shines in the sun, and just by slightly changing the angle of the head or moving the body a little they are able to transform themselves from one dazzling shade to another. As if this were not enough many also possess additional finery, like the White-booted Racquet-tail (*Ocreatus underwoodi*), which not only has legs covered by long downy feathers but also has long wire-like outer tail feathers, each with a racquet-like black feathered tip. Another tiny hummingbird, Gould's Heavenly Sylph (*Cyanolesbia coelestis*) has a purplish tail more than five inches long.

The hummingbird family is confined to the New World, ranging from Alaska in the north to Tierra del Fuego in the south, and is especially abundant in the subtropical parts of the South American Andes. The smallest species is the Bee Hummingbird (*Mellisuga helanae*) of Cuba, which including the bill and tail measures only a little more than two inches and is the world's smallest bird. Most species are slightly bigger than the Bee but smaller than the Giant Hummingbird (*Patagona gigas*) of the Andes, which measures eight and a half inches in length.

Hummingbirds feed on nectar from flowers and on tiny soft insects. To obtain the nectar they normally hover in front of a flower and probe their bill into it, or if the flower is particularly long they may pierce the side. To suit this mode of feeding they have long slender bills that are generally straight although some are downward curved and in a few instances they even curve upwards. The bill of the Sword-billed Hummingbird (*Ensifera ensifera*) is as long as the bird's entire head and body combined.

Not only can hummingbirds hover so that they remain stationary in the air, which they frequently do when feeding, but they are the only birds able to fly backwards. In

A Keel-billed Toucan, sometimes called Rainbow-billed. No really satisfactory explanation has been found for the grotesque size and brilliant mixed colours of the Toucan's beak; though it is not as cumbersome as it might seem as it is very light.

flight their wings may beat as many as eighty times per second, while around fifty beats per second is not uncommon.

A small, open, cup-shaped nest is built, made from cotton, moss, lichen, spiders' webs or similar materials, and placed on a twig or among foliage. Normally two white eggs are laid, and the young that are hatched blind and practically naked do not leave the nest until at least three weeks old. The nest building, incubation of the eggs, and rearing of the young are all undertaken by the female alone.

At a quick glance some of the jacamars, with their glittering plum-age and long, thin bills, could perhaps be mistaken for hummingbirds. They are however bigger, ranging from five inches in length up to the Great Jacamar (*Jacamerops aurea*), which is nearly a foot long. The latter ranges from Costa Rica to the Amazon.

Jacamars feed exclusively upon insects, which they usually capture in flight, and show a special liking for morphos and large swallowtail butterflies. They choose a perch that affords a good view, then sit looking from side to side until some unsuspecting winged insect flies by. The jacamar then darts off in pursuit, captures it and with the insect

Two birds which are instantly recognizable . . . above, this Mexican Macaw has the amusing face and knowing eye of all Parrots, and has perhaps an extra glint due to the fact that these Macaws are the most gaudy and brilliant of the parrot family. Right, one of the few parrots found in Africa is the Senegal Parrot. It has a grey head, shining sea-green bib, wings and back, and a golden orange stomach and is seen here about to eat the seeds of a huge sunflower.

still fluttering in the bill returns to the perch, against which it beats its catch until dead, before swallowing the body. Jacamars nest chiefly in burrows like the Old World bee-eaters, who also have similar feeding habits.

Motmots lack the brilliant colours of the previous group, and instead are clad in soft shades of green and rufous, with maybe a little bright blue colouring on the head. The family are confined to tropical America, where in some parts they are abundant. A notable feature of the more typical species is the tail, with its two especially long central feathers. When the bird first grows

these, after each moult, they are like most other feathers, but when they have been preened several times the subterminal portion falls away to expose a length of bare shaft and leave two racquet-like tips. When perched, motmots often swing their tails from side to side like a pendulum.

The name toucan comes from the word 'tucano' in the language of the Tupi Indians of Brazil, which is just one of the parts of tropical America inhabited by these colourful clowns of the bird world. The thirty seven or so species live in wooded country feeding on fruits, berries, various insects, and small animals. Because

of the enormous size of the bill, the bird achieves the seemingly difficult task of transferring food from the tip to the throat by tossing it into the air with a backwards jerk of the head, then catching and swallowing it. Although in some species the bill appears almost too heavy for the bird to support, it is in fact very light as the horny outer shell, often brightly coloured, is filled with a honeycomb-like cellular bony tissue.

Why do toucans have such large bills? One suggestion is that, because of their large body size, they need to perch on the thick, strong inner branches of trees, and the bill may help them to reach fruits growing

on the slender outer limbs. This would explain the bill's length, but not the exceptional shape or gay colours. It is possible that the colours and patterns serve as a form of recognition between species with similar plumage. As both male and female toucans possess brightly coloured bills it is unlikely that they play any major part in courtship display.

The largest species is the Toco Toucan (*Ramphastos toco*) which has a mainly orange bill with some red markings and a black patch at the

tip. Swainson's Toucan (*R. swainsonii*) has a diagonally marked bill, one portion being yellow the other dark red, while another species has a green bill with red, orange, and blue markings, and is often called the Rainbow-billed Toucan (*R. sulfuratus*). Ranging from southern Mexico to northern South America, the latter is also known as the Keel-billed Toucan. Some of the smaller members of the group are called toucanets and aracaris.

To the ancient Mayas and Aztecs, the Quetzal (*Pharomachrus mocino*),

which lives in mountain forests from southern Mexico to western Panama, was a sacred bird. Sometimes called the Resplendent Trogon, it is a most magnificent creature. The crested male is a brilliant shining green with decorative pointed feathers on the wing, and greatly elongated upper tail coverts that extend in a graceful curve far beyond the tip of the tail. His belly is vermilion and the underside of the tail pure white.

Along the overgrown banks of large rivers and their tributaries in

Left, a Long-tailed Sylph
Hummingbird hovers as only
Hummers can in order to drink from
a feeder hung out specially for them.

Below, a family of Rheas.
Sometimes called South American
Ostriches, they are the largest of the
New World birds, but are not in fact
related to or nearly as big as
Ostriches.

northern South America lives the strange Hoatzin. A lazy creature, it generally lives in groups of ten to twenty birds and is most active in the mornings and evenings and on moonlit nights. It feeds mainly on the tough leaves, flowers, and fruits of certain plants that grow in these marshy places, and exists only where they occur. To cope with this diet the Hoatzin possesses a peculiar digestive system, with the food being broken down not in the gizzard but in a much enlarged crop. The latter is situated high in the chest, so after a particularly big meal the Hoatzin has a very top-heavy appearance. To help keep balance as it crouches on a branch, the bird supports itself on its breastbone, which is covered by a pad of horny skin.

Measuring just over two feet in length, the Hoatzin has an extremely small head with an erect bristly crest, a long neck, and a small body with large loosely-held wings and a long broad tail. The plumage is mainly dark brown above and pale reddish-yellow below, and there is bare blue skin around the eye. The wing structure of the young Hoatzin recalls that of *Archaeopteryx*, for there are two claws on each wing

Above, Flamingoes.

Right, the Secretary Bird lives on the plains of southern Africa, and is a hawk of over four feet in height with long legs and distinctive plumes at the back of the head. It feeds on snakes, stamping on them with its feet or carrying them up into the air and then dropping them on hard ground to kill them.

which the bird uses for grasping while climbing about in branches. Should danger threaten, young Hoatzins drop into the water and, using both wings and legs, swim off, later climbing out again and continuing on their way through the branches. As it gets older the young Hoatzin loses its claws, but still continues to use its wings to help it climb about branches throughout its adult life.

Notable among the other species that share a similar habitat to the Hoatzin are the Scarlet Ibis (*Eudocimus ruber*) and the Boat-billed Heron (*Cochlearius cochlearius*), sometimes simply called the Boatbill. The Ibis, with its characteristic curved bill, is a gorgeous red, except for jet black wing tips. On account of this brilliant plumage it is relentlessly hunted and is much in demand by zoos throughout the world. Lacking any bright colours, the Boatbill

is mainly black and brown and stands only some 20 inches high. The peculiar bill, from which it takes its name, is broad and flattened and can be used to scoop for prey in shallow water.

James's Flamingo (*Phoenicoparrus jamesi*), the rarest of the flamingoes, was recently rediscovered in the Andes of Bolivia after having been thought to be almost extinct. Along with the Andean Flamingo (*P. andinus*), it lives in the high Andes on alkaline lakes at up to 14,000 feet. The Chilean Flamingo (*Phoenicopterus ruber chilensis*) inhabits temperate South America, while the American or Rosy species (*P. r. ruber*), which is becoming increasingly rare, is found on the Atlantic seaboard and islands of subtropical and tropical America.

Nearly all of the ninety-odd species that go to form the Cotinga family are confined to the tropical parts of

Central and South America, and range in size from that of a finch up to a crow. They are very diverse in appearance, some possessing brilliant or unusual colours while others have curiously modified feathers on the wing and head region, and yet others have peculiar fleshy wattles. Two species that fall into the latter category are the Mossy-throated and Three-wattled Bellbirds (*Procnias averano* and *P. tricarunculata*). The former has a mass of fine black fleshy wattles hanging like a beard from the throat, and the other has a long thin fleshy wattle on top of the bill and another hanging either side.

The Umbrella-bird (*Cephalopterus ornatus*) not only has a feathered wattle hanging from the throat which is as long as the bird itself, but a black umbrella-like crest. When it displays, the crest is spread to cover the whole top of the head, and the bird produces a rumbling sound.

Right, the Tanagers are a large and well-known family of brightly coloured little birds also living in the forests of Central and South America. The Blue-grey Tanager is one of the larger species and feeds on fruit and berries.

57

Above, a black and white Pied Kingfisher.

Left, the Crowned Cranes of Africa are some of the most distinctive members of a magnificent family, unfortunately all too badly in need of protection the world over. These tall stately birds live in marshes and swampy ground in large flocks and frequently utter very loud, trumpet-like calls to keep the flock together which can be heard for several miles.

modified wing feathers. They are visited by the females, who take part in a joint dance with them.

Manakins are tiny birds about the size of a tit, and are closely akin to the Cotingas. They are often attractively coloured, an example being the male Blue-backed Manakin (*Chiroxiphia pareola*), which has a deep red cap and blue back that contrasts sharply with the remainder of his plumage which is velvety black. Two males of this species will regularly dance side by side on a branch, jumping up and down alternately.

Africa

The African avifauna is very different from that found in Central and South America and the New World generally, with such birds as the Shoebill (*Balaeniceps rex*), Hammer-kop (*Scopus umbretta*), guineafowls, turacos, mousebirds, wood-hoopoes and the oxpeckers, which search the hides of large mammals for ticks, being particularly characteristic. Africa, from the southern fringes of the Sahara Desert, extending down to the South African Cape and along with the south-west corner of Arabia, is the home of the truly African birds. The species found in the parts of Africa north of the Sahara are more akin to those living in southern Europe.

Largest of the African birds, indeed the largest living bird, is the Ostrich (*Struthio camelus*). A fully grown male may stand nearly eight feet tall and weigh more than 300 pounds, while the female is slightly smaller. Chiefly a bird of the open plains, the Ostrich will often associate with zebras, antelopes, and giraffes. Not only is it wary but fleet of foot, or otherwise it could not have survived so long as it has on a continent where large predators abound. Its long neck enables it to spot danger long before most other plains dwelling creatures, while its powerful legs provide means for a speedy getaway. Nevertheless, this huge flightless bird was formerly more abundant than it is today. There is considerable doubt whether a few individuals of the northern Syrian race (*S. c. syriacus*) from Syria and Arabia may still survive, or if this bird is extinct.

Bright orange, the male Cock-of-the-rock (*Rupicola rupicola*), has an upright crest like an open fan which spreads from the nape to the bill and conceals the latter. Several males gather together at display grounds on the forest floor to show off.

In contrast to the Cock-of-the-rock, which adopts a static posture, sometimes held for several minutes, on its display arena, some of the manakins which have display grounds or leks are far more active. Gould's Manakin (*Manacus vitellinus*) normally finds a place in the forest which has at least one vertical sapling, then clears the ground around it by removing leaves and any other debris it is able to carry. The male dances and jumps about on the sapling, producing loud snapping and whirring noises with specially

Another bird very much at home in open country is the Secretary Bird (*Sagittarius serpentarius*). A long-legged bird of prey, it kills not just rodents and such-like but also snakes, some of them poisonous, the prey being dispatched by repeated blows from the foot. Now found only south of the Sahara, the Secretary Bird was once more widespread for fossil remains of it have been unearthed in France.

Probably the greatest bird spectacle to be seen in the world is the huge flocks of flamingoes that gather on the alkaline Rift Valley lakes of East Africa, especially Nakuru, Magadi, Natron, and Manyara. A visit to at least one of these lakes is usually included in the itinerary of every tourist who visits East Africa. These visitors have the thrill of seeing thousands of pink flamingoes honking, bathing, preening, squabbling, flying, and perhaps even displaying, while if they are particularly fortunate they may have the experience of seeing perhaps more than two million birds present on one lake at the same time. These enormous flocks are composed mainly of Lesser Flamingoes (*Phoeniconaias minor*) who greatly outnumber the bigger, paler Greater species (*Phoenicopterus ruber roseus*).

The Rift Valley lakes, some of which are freshwater, also provide a home for a multitude of other birds, not least the magnificent Fish Eagle (*Haliaetus vocifer*). Many waterfowl like the Cage Wigeon (*Anas capensis*) live on them, as do White and

Above, two Red-headed Lovebirds living up to their name.

Left, the Congo Peacock was only discovered thirty six years ago and it lives in the depths of the Congo forest. It is the first of the true Pheasants known from Africa and has handsome bronze and green plumage.

Pink-backed Pelicans (*Pelecanus onocrotalus* and *P. rufescens*), together with countless herons, egrets, cormorants, darters, and other water-birds. The Pied Kingfisher (*Ceryle rudis*) and tiny Malachite Kingfisher (*Corythornis cristata*) catch fish in their waters, and Crowned Cranes (*Balearica pavonina*) come to drink and nest along their shores.

Among the wealth of African birds there are few quite so extra-ordinary as the bare-headed rock-fowl, of which there are just two species, both similar in appearance to each other yet unlike any other bird. They are extremely graceful and alert creatures who seldom fly, but progress about the forest floor where they live by a series of hops on their long legs. The species

inhabiting Sierra Leone, Liberia, Ghana, and Togo is generally known as the White-necked Rockfowl (*Picathartes gymnocephalus*), and the other from Cameroun as the Grey-necked Rockfowl (*P. oreas*). Sometimes in the past they were called bald crows, but are now considered to be large specialized babblers.

For so large a bird their nesting habits are every bit as remarkable as their looks, for they build a mud nest like that of a swallow on a rockface deep in the forest. The mud, which is probably collected from a nearby stream, is interwoven with fibres and reinforced around the rim with small sticks. Owing to its large size the nest collapses easily when wet, and so must be built on the face of a rock with sufficient overhang to

Left, a Bronze Sunbird at its nest.

Right, this Superb Starling from Kenya is one of many different species of Starling to be found in Africa. It has brilliant emerald green and metallic blue plumage with orange underparts.

shelter it from the rain. As such sites are distinctly rare, it may be the lack of suitable nesting places that accounts for the birds' rarity. Recently, further dangers to its existence have been posed by the felling and destruction of their forest home, together with the collection of specimens for zoos and museums.

One of the last big mammals to be discovered was the Okapi, a shy creature that lives in the depths of the Congo forest. It was from this same rain forest that the Congo Peacock (*Afropavo congensis*) was first described as late as 1936. Even then the existence of it would not have been known had it not been for the sharp eyes of an American ornithologist who spotted a strange feather he was unable to identify in the headdress of a pygmy. He spent

years following up this very slender clue until eventually his hard work was rewarded with the discovery of a living peacock.

The Grey Parrot (*Psittacus erithacus*) lives in the forests of most of tropical Africa, feeding on all kinds of seeds and fruits. Surprisingly few parrots occur in Africa but this bird, which lacks the gaudy plumage of many tropical American species, being grey with a red tail, is perhaps best known of them all. Popular as a cage bird it makes a splendid pet, with a wonderful ability to mimic human speech and other sounds.

Like the Grey Parrot the tiny lovebirds also enjoy considerable popularity as cage and aviary birds. They lack the ability to talk but do possess colourful plumage, with green, red, and yellow being particu-

larly prominent. It is the affection paired birds show to each other that accounts for their name.

Turacos, mousebirds and wood-hoopoes are three groups found nowhere but south of the Sahara. Of the trio the turacos are the largest group both in number of species and actual body size. They inhabit many different types of country ranging from dry thorn bush to rain forest. Most are principally green while two are violet-blue, five mainly grey, and another, aptly named the Great Blue Turaco (*Corythaeola cristata*), is much larger. The green and violet-blue species are remarkable in that they possess crimson flight feathers which contain a substance known as turacin. Once it was widely believed the red could be washed out of the feathers by rain, but this has now been proved incorrect, although it can be dissolved by an alkali.

Sometimes called colies, the six species of mousebirds are all dull brown or grey, with a crest and long tapering tail. Some have red legs and feet, as well as bare red or blue skin around the eye, while others lack even these modest embellishments. It is the mouse-like way they creep among thick foliage in search of fruits and berries that gives rise to their unusual name, and where fruit is grown they are often persecuted because of the damage they cause. The common and widespread Speckled Mousebird (*Colius striatus*) is found throughout most of the continent south of the Sahara.

Kakelaars, as the wood-hoopoes are alternatively known, have blackish plumage, glossed green, purple, or blue, and a long tapered tail. The slender, slightly curved bill is used to probe among the trunks and branches of trees for grubs and insects. Usually wood-hoopoes travel about in small family parties, attracting attention with their noisy chattering.

Anybody encountering starlings in Africa for the first time cannot help but be amazed, not only at their brilliant colours but also by the astonishing variety of species. Of these beautiful birds none surpass the Golden-breasted Starling (*Cosmopsarus regius*), a species sometimes called, justifiably, the Royal Starling. Found only in Ethiopia, Somalia, Tanzania and eastern Kenya, it lives in dry bush country and is particularly fond of feeding on termites.

At Kilaguni Lodge in Tsavo National Park, Kenya, this species and the more numerous Superb Starling (*Spreo superbus*), in the company of hornbills and weavers, will come to visitors' tables at mealtimes to collect scraps.

Living only in a small area of West Africa is a rare and little known species, the Emerald Starling (*Lamprotornis iris*), which is every bit as beautiful as the others being a lovely glossy green and purple.

Although they occur throughout most tropical parts of the Old World from Africa eastwards to Australia, the sunbirds are to be seen in greatest profusion in Africa. They are in many respects counterparts of the New World hummingbirds, for like the latter they are tiny creatures with glittering plumage that feed

principally on nectar obtained from flowers, and on insects.

The Beautiful Sunbird (*Nectarinia pulchella*) is particularly fond of the flowers of aloes and acacia blossoms, and usually feeds from a perched position like other sunbirds, who unlike hummingbirds rarely hover. Outside the breeding season the male Beautiful Sunbird, in common with some other species, loses his colourful dress which is replaced by a more sober garb like that of his mate. Most female sunbirds lack metallic feathering and are dull shades of green, yellow, brown or grey, although some like the female Collared Sunbird (*Anthreptes collaris*) closely resemble the mate.

Similar to the sunbirds in general build and habits are the Cape Sugarbird (*Promerops cafer*) and Natal Sugarbird (*P. gurneyi*), the sole members of a group that is confined to the most southern parts of the continent. Chiefly brown with a long tail they lack any metallic feathering and are not related to the sunbirds but probably to the Australasian honeyeaters.

Whereas most birds attempt to conceal their nests, weavers generally do quite the reverse for their nests, which can be encountered, sometimes in huge numbers, festooning the branches of trees over much of Africa. Usually globular-shaped, they are frequently elaborately woven affairs made from vegetable fibres. To afford protection the nests are usually suspended from the extremities of branches or palm fronds, often over water or close to human habitations. Access to some nests is by means of a long entrance tube, perhaps two feet long, hanging from the underside.

Like the Village or Black-headed Weaver (*Ploceus cucullatus*) that commonly nests in and around towns and villages, particularly in West Africa, most species are predominantly yellow and black, while some, but by no means all, females are dull streaky-looking birds. Others, like the male Red-crowned Bishop (*Euplectes hordeaceus*), are red and black. The Red-billed Quelea (*Quelea quelea*) is such a serious pest to grain in agricultural areas that attempts to control it include such extreme measures as

Above, the nests of the Blackcapped Social Weavers – often whole trees are covered in these large balls of woven grasses and sticks.

Left, the Cape Sugar Bird feeds on nectar like the Sunbirds and has a remarkably long tail – on the male it measures sixteen to seventeen inches.

aeriel spraying with poisons, and blowing up its roosting places.

An astonishing communal nesting structure, sometimes as big as a small hut, is built by the Social Weaver (*Philetairus socius*). Each pair has its own nesting chamber and all the occupants together build and repair the communal roof over the colony. One such dwelling that has been described contained ninety-five nests.

Like the cuckoo, whydahs lay their eggs in the nests of other birds, leaving the foster-parents to raise the young. The widespread Paradise Whydah (*Vidua paradisea*) lays its eggs in the nest of the Green-winged Pytilia (*Pytilia melba*), and in southern Africa the Shaft-tailed Whydah (*V. regia*) parasitizes the Violet-eared Waxbill (*Granatina granatina*).

Not to be confused with the whydahs are the somewhat similar, but bigger, widow-birds. They are not parasitic, but the males are polygamous and may have a harem of six or more females. Resplendent in black, with orange-red shoulder patches, the male Long-tailed Widow-bird (*Euplectes progne*) has a magnificent full black tail some twenty inches long, which ripples behind as he flies.

Despite the nearness of Madagascar many birds found in Africa do not occur there, while a number of birds are unique to the island. Three families found nowhere else are the mesites, the asitys and false sunbirds, and the vangas or vanga-shrikes. Some, like the Madagascar Bee-eater (*Merops superciliosus*) and Broad-billed Roller (*Eurystomus glaucurus*), live in both Africa and Madagascar, and regularly migrate across the Mozambique Channel.

Birds of prey

IAN PRESTT

The term 'Birds of Prey' has no precise scientific basis, but is a popular expression used to describe fierce birds which usually feed on live prey which they seize with their talons. It can invariably be taken to include all the diurnal species, such as the eagles, hawks and falcons (more precisely described as 'raptors') and it may or may not also include the mainly nocturnal owls. For convenience, in the present work, both groups have been included in the same chapter, but this does not necessarily mean that they are closely related. The conclusive evidence required to decide this question one way or another has yet to be found.

The Raptors

This group contains some of the most magnificent birds known to Man. Their impressive appearance – fierce eyes, strong hooked beak, powerful talons – and exceptional powers of flight, at once distinguishes them from all other birds. Man has in fact long recognized their unique characteristics as symbols of power and strength. In Ancient Egypt there were many falcon gods, and pairs of falcons were worshipped in the temples and falcons were buried in predynastic tombs. The chiefs of hunting tribes, such as those of the North American Red Indians, decorated their head-dress and spears with bird of prey feathers, particularly those of the eagle, both to testify to their rank and to endow themselves with the virtues of avian hunters. The warriors wore eagle feathers in their hair, the number indicating their prowess in battle. In more recent civilizations, the eagle and falcon have appeared again and again in all parts of the world on the banners of nations and on the flags and badges of armies; and recently have been frequently employed as monograms by business corporations, such as banks and insurance companies, to indicate strength and reliability. A further association between man and the birds of prey arises through the ancient art of falconry, in which eagles, falcons and hawks of several species are trained to fly from the fist at wild prey.

Size

In general, as one would expect, birds of prey are large as they have to be able to capture and kill live prey. However their size varies considerably and corresponds to the differing sizes and types of prey, which ranges from insects to quite large mammals. At one extreme there are two species of condor in the Americas, with a wing span of up to ten feet and a weight of over twenty pounds, which are amongst the largest flying birds in the world. At the other end of the scale there are the tiny falconets, found from India to the Philippines, which are only about six inches long and weigh

The Cooper's Hawk has the typical rounded wings, long tail and quick dashing flight of all the Hawks, and is one of the species most popularly used for falconry. This bird is wearing 'jesses' by which he is attached to his perch.

one-tenth of a pound.

In the vast majority of raptors the female is larger than the male. This difference is most pronounced in the aggressive, fast flying species, such as the larger falcons and the hawks, for example the female Goshawk (*Accipiter gentilis*) can be almost twice the size of the male. The reason for this difference is not at all clear; possibly the female needs to protect the young from the male in a naturally ferocious and predacious species; or it may be an important factor in enabling such fierce and solitary birds to pair up and not regard each other as competitors. Finally it may mean that the pair can have a greater range of the prey available within their nesting territory, at the time when they have young in the nest and considerable quantities of food are required in limited hunting time.

Plumage and Colouration

The colouration of the birds of prey is in general rather subdued, though many are extremely handsome as a result of a very extensive range of browns, blended in an almost infinite variety of forms with black, grey and white. Barring, streaking and spotting are common and frequently take the form of a bold distinctive feature, such as the moustache-like stripes

Above, a Hen Harrier at its nest. The male has attractive soft grey plumage, the female is a dark brown and has streaked underparts. Rather than having good eyesight like most of the birds of prey, Harriers have excellent hearing, and their large ear openings are protected by feather ruffs giving them their owl-like appearance.

Right, Kestrels are among the fastest of all birds of prey and are the most numerous of all the falcons in Europe. This one has just caught a vole and has returned to a rock to eat it.

found in some of the falcons. The upper-parts in most species are darker than the under-parts and the under-surfaces of the wings and tail are commonly barred. The brightest colours are usually present in the eye and legs, which are commonly bright yellow or less often red. In many of the vultures, the characteristic featherless part of the head also has the skin brightly coloured and in some the effect is further enhanced by the addition of wattles.

In most species the sexes are alike in their colouration, though in some, such as hawks of the genus *Accipiter* and many of the falcons, particularly the Merlin (*Falco columbarius*), the male is bluer. This feature is seen in its most extreme form in the harriers (*Circus spp.*); the adult male Hen Harrier (*C. cyaneus*), is an almost unmarked bluey-grey and white in striking contrast to the heavily marked brown females. In some of the kestrels (*Falco spp.*) the different colouration between the sexes is confined to only certain parts of the body, such as the head, tail or wings, one or more of these regions taking on a bluish tinge in the adult male plumage. Thus in the Common Kestrel (*Falco tinnunculus*) the head and tail of the male are bright blue, while those of the female are brown; but in the male American Kestrel (*Falco sparverius*) the wing coverts and head are blue, while in the female the head only is blue.

A number of species are crested, and these crests vary in size, from the only slightly enlarged nape feathers of the *Accipiterine* hawks (which however have white bases to the nape feathers, so when raised these nevertheless stand out in marked contrast to the darker plumage of the crown) to the greatly extended nape feathers of the African Long-crested Eagle (*Lophoaetus occipitalis*), which hang forward over its head. Some like the Harpy Eagle (*Harpia harpyja*) and the Crowned Eagle (*Stephanoaetus coronatus*) have a crest which is fully divided into two. The birds raise their crests in anger and not in their courtship displays which usually take place in the air.

Individuals of the same species can vary considerably in colour and

markings even in the same locality, for instance the Common Buzzard (*Buteo buteo*) and the Rough-legged Buzzard (*B. lagopus*) can vary in colour from extremely pale white and grey to almost black, and some specimens of the normally brown Red-tailed Hawk (*Buteo jamaicensis*) and Ferroginous Hawk (*B. regalis*) of America have chestnut or rufous plumage. In the Gyr Falcon (*Falco rusticolus*) individuals of the so-called white phase predominate in the High Arctic, while the dark phase birds which have heavily barred, grey plumage become more common as one moves south. In this case the plumage differences are more correctly termed geographic variation.

Young birds of prey are covered in down and remain in the nest for a period of several weeks or some-times months until the down is replaced by the first (juvenile) plumage. The juveniles tend to have pale orange-buff or white tips to the feathers of the back, wings and tail, and the feathers of their underparts are usually darker than those of the adults and tend to be streaked and blotched rather than barred. In some species such as Cooper's Hawk (*Accipiter cooperii*) of America and the Peregrine (*Falco peregrinus*), some of the juvenile feathers are longer than the equivalent feathers in the adult, giving the younger birds a bulkier appearance. The first of the juvenile feathers to be moulted are those of the body, which are replaced by a partial moult in the autumn of the year of birth. The wing and tail feathers are not shed until the late summer of the following year when the bird is just over a

Above, a Buzzard brings a rabbit to the nest.

Right, the large Andean Condor has a wing span of nine to ten feet and is a very strong bird able to kill sick or sleeping llamas and horses if it is really hungry.

year old, and by this time these feathers are frequently extremely worn and faded. Most raptors can be said to be in mature plumage when about three years old, although it varies according to their size.

Evolution and Classification
Classification, which ideally should follow an evolutionary sequence, has proved extremely difficult in the case of the raptors. Like all the main groups of birds they evolved at a very early stage after the appearance of the first true birds – a generalized bird of prey is known from Eocence deposits laid down about seventy-five thousand years ago. Additional difficulties to establish a classification arise from the lack of fossil evidence, and because of the similarity of so many of the present day families as a result of convergent evolution within the group as a whole. Separation of one species from another has had to be based therefore on mainly superficial differences.

The raptors form the scientific Order *Falconiformes*. This Order can be conveniently sub-divided into three Sub-Orders: *Cathartae* – the New World vultures; *Falcones* – the falcon-like raptors; and *Accipitres* – the hawk-like raptors. They are found throughout the world and there are altogether about 280 species living today.

The New World Vultures
(Cathartae)
There are only six living species included in this group, all of which are confined to the New World; and the best known are the very large Andean Condor (*Vultur gryphus*) and California Condor (*Gymnogyps californianus*). The latter previously ranged from Washington State south to northern California, but is now becoming increasingly rare and is restricted to the southern coastal ranges of California. They all have

featherless heads, very large broad wings and a well developed sense of smell, presumably to help them locate the carrion on which they feed. The toes and claws, as one would expect, are not strongly developed, the hind two in particular being weak and small. They do not build nests and the smaller vultures lay two eggs while the condors lay only one every other year as the young birds take so long to rear. Their calls consist of grunts and hisses.

The Falcon-like Raptors
(*Falcones*)

The majority of falcons are highly adapted to an open habitat and swift flight to overtake other birds and, apart from a difference in size, they represent a remarkably uniform group, the sub-divisions of which still have not been satisfactorily worked out. Because of this the entire Sub-Order is included within one Family *Falconidae* with four Sub-Families: (i) the caracaras (*Polyborinae*) (ii) the laughing and forest falcons (*Herpetotherinae*) (iii) the pigmy falcons (*Polihieracinae*) (iv) the true falcons (*Falconidae*).

The caracaras are scavengers with weak, only slightly hooked bills, weak legs and almost straight claws, and may well provide an indication of the appearance of the more primitive ancestral stock from which the true falcons evolved. The ten known species are mainly found in South America and in size range from a length of fifteen to twenty two inches. There is only one species of Laughing Falcon (*Herpetotheres cachinnans*), a snake-feeding falcon of Mexico and central America. The forest falcons are a group of five species highly adapted to life in the tropical forests of the New World and because of this forest habit are unlike other falcons in having short, rounded wings and thin legs more reminiscent of forest-living hawks. The falconets comprise eight or nine species of small falcons, mostly only about six inches in length, and which prey on insects and small birds.

The group to which the name 'true falcons' has been given, contains the best known and most highly evolved of the falcon-like

birds. There are about thirty five species (doubt over the precise number arising from the difficulty of deciding which are good species and which are simply geographical races), and they are all included in the single Genus *Falco*. In flight they display a characteristic silhouette, resulting from their large heads, broad shoulders, long pointed wings and longish tail. The biggest is the Gyr Falcon (*F. rusticolus*) which can go up to twenty four inches and weigh twenty pounds, while the smallest is the Seychelles Kestrel (*F. araea*) of only eight or nine inches length and weighing six oz. The typical falcon is about twelve inches in length and has a round, blunt head, short neck and dark moustache-like stripes running from the edges of its mouth. The short hooked bill is conspicuously 'toothed' in the upper mandible, with a corresponding notch in the lower one. The eye is large and dark,

the body streamlined and covered with hard, compact feathers. The legs are usually short and thick, the toes powerful and – especially the middle one – often long with sharp claws. The colouration of the upper-parts is often grey and that of the under-parts rufous dark brown.

There are several more or less distinct groups contained within the Genus. The kestrels (ten species) have a characteristic mode of hunting by hovering high in the air before plunging down to kill, and include a high proportion of small mammals, reptiles and ground-dwelling insects in their diets. They are found throughout the world and are mainly solitary and sedentary, nesting on ledges, in cavities or in old nests of other species (the two exceptions are the Lesser Kestrel (*F. naumanni*) and the Red-footed Falcon (*F. vespertinus*) which nest in colonies). A second group is the merlins (two species), typified by

the Halarctic Merlin (*F. columbarius*). It is a small dashing falcon, often used in falconry, and usually nests on the ground on moorland.

A third contains the hobbies, about twelve species of very long-winged falcons renowned for their swift flight. Most of their prey is caught in full flight and includes a high proportion of flying insects as well as small birds. They occur throughout the world and being highly insectivorous it is not unexpected to find that half the species are migratory. A fourth group contains the great falcons, which are the most impressive falcons by virtue of their size, all being over seventeen inches. Included in this group are the Lanner (*F. biarmicus*), Prairie (*F. mexicanus*), Saker (*F. cherrug*), Lagger (*F. jugger*) and Gyr (*F. rusticolus*) falcons.

The fifth and last group contains the peregrines, all highly specialized for preying on flying birds which

Above, the most regal and awe inspiring bird in existence, the Golden Eagle, lives in wild mountainous regions across Eurasia and North America, but is now rarely seen due to the shooting by 'sportsmen'.

Left, the magnificent fish-eating Osprey is the size of a small eagle but has long and narrow wings so that it can plunge into water after its prey.

Right, Buzzards are the small relations of the Eagles and are numerous in most parts of the world. They can be easily identified by their very blunt, rounded wings with feathered tips. This is a Rough-legged Buzzard and is found over most low arctic regions.

Above, Merlins are the smallest of the European Falcons and are fast, low level hunters in open country.

Left, a young Peregrine wearing jesses round his legs as part of his training by a falconer. Peregrines kill other flying birds by plunging down with great speed and accuracy from high above and knocking them to the ground with one blow.

Right, the largest owl is the European Eagle Owl. The attractive tufts which look like ears in fact have nothing to do with the bird's hearing and many other owls also have these distinctive feathers.

Above, a Red Kite and its young, one of the very few families left in Britain. Kites are not so fast or ferocious as hawks and falcons and are well adapted to gliding.

Left, it is hard to believe that this maternal looking bird is the largest and most ferocious of the true Hawks, and is expert at flying through woodland in pursuit of its prey which it kills by the powerful grip of its needle sharp talons. It is a Northern Goshawk and is found throughout Northern temperate regions.

they grasp or knock to the ground at the end of a tremendous stoop. The Peregrine (*F. peregrinus*) is one of the most widely distributed and successful birds in the world and no less than eighteen races are recognized, differing slightly from each other in size and colour. It is territorial and solitary, usually nesting in a traditional eyrie on a cliff ledge. Throughout history they have proved to be the most outstanding species to train for the purposes of falconry.

The Hawk-like Raptors
(*Accipitres*)
This Sub-Order contains three Families: the largest *Accipitridae* includes the most familiar birds of this group – the kites, hawks, eagles

and Old World vultures; the other two *Pandionidae* and *Sagittariidae* each only contain a single species – the Osprey (*Pandion haliaetus*) and the Secretary Bird (*Sagittarius serpentarius*) respectively.

The Osprey and the Secretary Bird are of particular interest as both feed almost exclusively on rather unusual prey; the Osprey on fish, and the Secretary Bird on snakes, scorpions and lizards. The Osprey is the size of a small eagle, but unlike eagles has rather long and narrow wings. When hunting it hovers about 50 to 100 feet over the water and then suddenly plunges in, more often than not emerging with a fish carried head forward in its feet. The lower surface of their toes are covered with sharp points which help them to hold the slippery prey. They have a distinctive appearance, with dark-brown upper-parts, white underneath, a white head with a broad black line running back from the forehead through the eye, and greenish-white legs. It occurs throughout the world and created considerable interest in Great Britain recently when it returned to breed in Scotland in 1959 after being absent for fifty years. Its numbers are currently declining in some parts of North America, apparently because of the persistent use of organochlorine pesticides.

The Secretary Bird, in contrast to the Osprey, is more restricted in its distribution, being confined to the plains of the southern half of Africa. It is essentially a grey coloured hawk, and stands four feet tall on long powerful legs that are heavily armoured against snake bites. It is distinguished by a long black crest and two very long central tail feathers that hang down far beyond the rest of the tail. They often hunt in pairs, and run at the prey at times beating their wings on the ground to distract it, and then using their feet to pin the snake to the ground, they kill it by battering it to death. Large snakes are carried

into the air and then dropped to kill them.

As previously mentioned, it seems not unreasonable to suppose that the raptors evolved from carrion-feeding birds. If this is correct the kites, many of which feed on carrion or simple prey such as insects and snails, probably most resemble the ancestral stock of the hawk-like birds. Next in evolutionary succession would have been the harriers, then the true-hawks, the buzzards and finally the eagles. The so-called booted eagles, which include some of the finest and most powerful of the eagles in the *Genus Aquila*, together with some of the larger falcons, are probably the most highly evolved birds of prey.

The typical kite is a medium sized bird with long wings and tail, well adapted to gliding and possessing little of the dash and ferocity of the falcons, hawks and eagles. There are some thirty one species found in many parts of the world. With the advance of civilization many of the carrion-feeders have decreased in numbers, and until the Middle Ages the Red Kite (*Milvus milvus*) was once common throughout Britain, but is now reduced to about two dozen pairs in the mountains of central Wales. Some kites have forked tails, this development being found in its most extreme form in the Swallow-tailed Kites of America and Africa, in which the deeply forked tail is as long again as the head and body. Some have very specialized feeding habits, such as the so-called Honey Buzzards (*Pernis spp.*) which feed almost exclusively on the larvae of wasps and bees and have densely feathered heads to protect them against the stings; while the Everglade Kite of southern Florida (*Rostrhamus sociabilis*) has a long, slender, sickle-shaped beak which enables it to feed on freshwater snails.

The Old World vultures, of which there are about fifteen species in all, superficially resemble the New World vultures already discussed, although the two groups differ markedly from each other in their detailed anatomy. They probably represent a specialized offshoot from the kites and differ from them in possessing very broad wings and

short tails, with which they are able to sail aloft for hours on end with few flaps. Most have the same, rather ugly head, devoid of feathers and often brightly coloured.

The harriers, of which there are ten species in one Genus *Circus*, are a characteristic cosmopolitan group of medium-sized raptors, possessing long, narrow wings, a long, rounded tail and an owl-like face. They occupy a wide variety of open habitats over which they hunt at low level, with a leisurely flapping and gliding flight, in search of small ground prey. They probably gave rise to the true hawks.

The true hawks, usually called sparrow-hawks and goshawks, comprise some fifty species, the vast majority being included in the Genus *Accipiter*. They represent some of the pluckiest and most dashing of the raptors. Most of them have short, broad wings and a long tail enabling them to fly at high speeds with incredible agility through woodland in pursuit of their prey. This is often other birds, which are caught either in full flight or from the ground or a branch. To help them snatch their prey, many have long slender legs and exceptionally long thin toes with needle-sharp talons. The largest and most ferocious is the Northern Goshawk (*A. gentilis*) which occurs in both the New and the Old World. The female can be up to twenty three inches in length and have a wing span of thirty three inches. The prey, which includes hares, squirrels, the young of foxes and wild cats, and large birds such as the Capercallie and Woodpigeon, is killed by the powerful grip of the talons which frequently pierce the victims neck. Many species of these true hawks have been used for falconry.

The two remaining groups of the hawk-like raptors, the buzzards and eagles, are somewhat similar in that both are large, have large broad wings and are renowned for their soaring flight. Unlike the vultures, however, their soaring flight can end in a steep dive and swerving chase to secure living prey – most often mammals and reptiles, but sometimes also birds. In these dives eagles have been known to reach a speed of over 100 miles an hour. Buzzards are about twenty inches long and have a wing span of three to five feet, while eagles can go up to a length of over three feet, have a wing span of six feet and weigh over ten pounds. Eagles in particular present a most magnificent appearance, with their massive beaks and immensely powerful talons which can readily pierce the hand of a man (even the thick leather gauntlet worn by a falconer often fails to protect them from a nasty wound). Many of these birds are hardy and well adapted to survive in harsh mountain habitats and at great

Far left, a Night Jar hovers while waiting to catch insects. They sleep during the day either in trees or on the ground and are so perfectly camouflaged that they have no fear until actually touched.

Below, a Marsh Harrier alighting at its nest.

heights, and in these northerly conditions they are usually the successful competitor with other mountain species such as the Peregrine and Raven (*Corvus corax*). They have the ability to survive for days without food, when conditions are too severe to enable them to hunt. Most eagles do not begin to breed until they are three or four years old, and in the wild they have been known to live for up to twenty years, while in captivity they have lived for over forty years.

The Owls

The owls resemble the raptors in many ways: both possess strong talons, hooked beaks and keen eyesight, and many species of both groups have the same habits. This resemblance could have evolved as a result of their both living in a similar environment and in the same way, and does not necessarily mean

that the two groups are closely related. As both raptors and owls hunt and catch the same prey in a similar fashion, it can easily be seen how during the course of time they could come to resemble each other.

Owls are in fact probably most closely related to the Oil Bird (*Steatornithidae*), the frog-mouths (*Pordargidae*), and the nightjars (*Caprimulogidae*). All of these birds (like the owls) are nocturnal, and they have a similar softish plumage and colouration (in the owls the plumage is remarkably soft, including the wing feathers, and they are able to fly with almost complete silence). Although both the raptors and owls are flesh-eaters, their anatomy is quite different. The blind-gut or caecum in raptors is practically vestigeal, on the other hand owls have a well-developed caeca (shaped rather like a Florence-flask) a distinct characteristic they

Above, a female Snowy Owl. These are large, striking birds that live on the arctic tundras. They have unusual nesting habits as they choose an open spot on high ground so as to keep an eye on the surrounding country.

Right, a Barn Owl flies home with a mouse. Notice the heart-shaped face and the long legs which are characteristics peculiar to Barn Owls.

share with nightjars. Another important difference between the raptors and the owls is that while nestling owls only have one set of down proceeding the feathers, the nestling raptor has two.

A unique characteristic of the owls is their eyes. These look directly forward and have little power of movement, so the birds have constantly to twist their necks, which they can do through an angle of 180°, in order to keep an all-round look out. Their round, flat faces are presumably an adaptation to their nocturnal habits, but nothing is more peculiar about owls than their ears. Although some species have ears like other birds, most of them have ears which are much enlarged and asymmetrical. The reason for this difference in size, associated as it is with other differences in the ear, is not known, but again it is assumed to be an adaptation to their nocturnal habit.

The outer toe in the owls is reversible, so they often perch with two toes to the front and two to the rear of the branch. This feature is not unique, however, since ospreys, woodpeckers (*Picidae*) and parrots (*Psittacidae*) all have the same thing. There are about 134 species of owls, but these have been further subdivided into over 350 sub-species. Some authorities divide the owls into two Families: the *Strigidae* – the typical or brown (123 species) and the *Tytonidae* – the barn-owls (11 species). The distinction between the two is however somewhat arbitrary and rests largely on the comb-like quality of the middle claw and the lighter colouration of the barn-owls.

In general appearance the owls form a very uniform group, being medium-sized (on average about sixteen inches in length), with longish, rather narrow wings, a short tail and legs feathered to the toes. In flight they quarter low over the ground with a slow flapping flight, alternated with gliding and perching – usually in an upright posture. During the day they roost in trees, old buildings and crevices in the rocks.

The largest owl is the European

Above, an angry owl is an intimidating sight with its glaring eyes, fluffed out feathers and snapping bill, and it can be dangerous when it attacks. This is a Short-eared Owl which is widespread throughout the Northern Hemisphere and is a highly migratory species.

Right, an adult Tawny Owl squeezing into its nesting hole. The Tawny is the owl most often seen and heard in Britain.

Eagle-owl (*Bubo bubo*), which has an overall length of twenty eight inches. It is a solitary bird occupying a variety of habitats, but preferring rocky promontaries in forests. Its food includes hares, hedgehogs, rats, mice and a variety of birds the size of a crow and larger. Another large owl is the Snowy Owl (*Nyctea scandiaca*). This bird is somewhat unusual in its distribution, being largely confined to cold northerly regions above the limit of trees. Appropriate to this wintry habitat the males are almost pure white, while the females are barred and spotted.

Some of the smaller owls are only five inches in length and these feed largely on insects. Many of them nest on the ground in burrows, well known examples being the Burrowing Owl (*Speotyto cunicularia*) of the Americas and the Little Owl (*Anethene noctua*) of Europe. Owls in general feed on mammals and roosting birds, and catch their prey with their talons, though they usually kill it with their beaks. Certain species have adopted specialized feeding techniques, in some cases including fish in their diet. The most extreme example of this being the remarkable Fishing-owl (*Scotopelia peli*) of Africa, which is a rather rare, large bird, and usually lives in pairs, in dense riverside trees.

Like that of the raptors, the colouration of owls tends to be of greys and brown, beautifully barred and spotted, forming a variety of shades and patterns. A characteristic of many owls is the tufts of feathers on the front of the head, which resemble ears. In all cases these have no connection with the true ears and play no function in the detection of sound. Nevertheless they are often quite striking in appearance when fully erect and give the name to many species, for example the Long-eared Owl, the Short-eared Owl and the Greathorned Owl.

The owls form a remarkable and interesting group of birds and in general are beneficial to man as many feed on pests such as rats and mice. Unfortunately they are still all too often persecuted, even though in most countries they are now protected by law.

85

Migration

DR JOHN SPARKS

Early Theories

The appearance and disappearance of certain kinds of birds with the changing of the seasons has always been a subject of comment and speculation; early observers were, however, at a loss to explain the phenomenon. An old sixteenth century illustration shows fishermen working a net containing both fish and birds, which was presumably in accordance with the then popular belief that swallows overwintered in the bottom of ponds. Others thought that cuckoos turned into hawks. Another theory was that in Autumn birds flew to the moon, an idea as preposterous as it was quaint, and one which should have been finally exploded by the observations of the Apollo astronauts!

What is Migration

Although there is one species which does hibernate the winter away – the North American Poor-will (a nightjar or night hawk) – it is now well known that the seasonal coming and going of some species is due to the fact that their populations have two home ranges; a breeding range, and one which they occupy outside the breeding season. These ranges may overlap to some extent, but this does not alter the situation; *migration* is the bi-annual movement of populations of birds between their breeding and non-breeding ranges. Other mass movements of birds, such as those due to hard

weather, irruptions and nomadic dispersal, will not be referred to here.

Migratory species that breed in the Northern hemisphere tend to move southwards to spend their off seasons in warm areas, some near, or even south of the equator. In the Southern hemisphere the reverse is true; the Long-tailed Cuckoo nests in New Zealand between October and March (the southern spring and summer), and then flies northwards to Melanesia where it spends the rest of the year. An exception to these patterns is the dainty Ross's Gull, which spends the winter in the Arctic seas and migrates *south* to breed on the well wooded marshes of Siberian rivers, a movement that is more characteristic of southern hemisphere species.

Not all birds take strongly lateral migratory flights. Arctic Warblers, small leaf warblers inhabiting birch and coniferous forests as far west as Arctic Norway, travel to SE Asia after the breeding season. Similarly, the Siberian race of the Willow Warbler flies 8,000 miles across Asia to winter in East Africa, a remarkable journey for a bird weighing less than half an ounce.

Incidentally, not all migrations involve flying. Rockhopper and Macaroni Penguins make regular northerly migrations from their rookery sites, and both the Adelie and Emperor Penguins may have to walk and toboggan over tens of

Bramblings resting in a tree during migration. They are a close relative of the Chaffinch and migrate rather erratically, sometimes in tremendous numbers exceeding several millions of birds.

Above, Curlews breed in the northern Tundra and migrate in winter, frequently going across the Equator. In the foreground are Oyster Catchers.

Left, the Arctic Tern is another bird that travels the most remarkable distances, and is perhaps the most famous migrant of all.

miles of sea ice to reach their nesting sites in the early Antarctic spring.

Long Distance Travellers

Many species make transequatorial journeys of staggering proportions. The most impressive of the world's long distance travellers is surely the Arctic Tern, a species that has an extensive breeding range in northern Europe and North America. Those that breed as far north as latitude 82°N travel down the Atlantic coast of Europe and Africa to the Antarctic seas at 74°S. The round trip is at least 22,000 miles as the 'crow' flies – but of course terns do not fly in straight lines! Equally impressive is the route taken by the Sharp-tailed Shearwaters or Muttonbirds (relatives

of the Manx Shearwater), which breed on small islands around Tasmania, and also cover about 22,000 miles a year. In much the same way, Giant Petrels and many Albatrosses spend their lives circumnavigating the globe in the teeth of the 'roaring forties' and other trade winds. The migration routes of the migratory European birds of prey and many White Storks tend to converge on the Near East because they are efficient soarers, not long distance flappers, and so tend to avoid crossing the Mediterranean Sea where there are no thermals to assist them. In autumn, 6,650 Honey Buzzards have been counted crossing the Bosphorus, near Istanbul, in a single day.

Some land based birds are also

great travellers. The Pacific Golden Plover nests in the Alaskan tundra, and winters in Hawaii and Tonga, 2,000 miles away in the central Pacific, thus requiring not only stamina but also very accurate navigation. Needle-tailed swifts bi-annually make the 6,000 or 7,000 mile journey between their breeding grounds in Siberia and Australia where they spend their off season.

Why Migrate?

The value of migration to certain birds is not too difficult to understand. By migrating, some birds are able to take advantage of food supplies that are only seasonally abundant in certain areas. It seems that the more temperate and tropical areas can provide a stable and reliable food supply throughout the year, so species that nest there do not need to emigrate in their off season. Migration is thus a phenomenon that tends to be associated with birds that nest in the higher latitudes.

This is particularly true for insectivorous birds. In late autumn and winter, insects are in short supply over much of Northern Europe, Asia and North America, but in spring there is a glut. Therefore by moving in at this time of the year, a host of chats, warblers, martins, flycatchers, etc. can exploit this rich source of food to rear their ravenous youngsters. Similarly, the plankton and land flora bloom, encouraging an increased fish and mammal population respectively. At the same time wildfowl, seabirds, raptors and many other small perching birds move northwards to breed, and after they have nested, when the days draw shorter, have to travel south again or else starve. Migration thus takes place for reasons of survival in these high latitudes. The survival value of long distance, transequatorial migrations therefore becomes evident; they enable some species to live in a perpetual summer of plenty!

European swallows, having raised perhaps two broods in the northern summer, spend the remainder of their year recuperating 5,000 miles away in the South African summer, where insects are still plentiful. Although they may seem incredible to us, the fantastic journeys of the Muttonbird and Arctic tern are, despite the energy they use, in the birds' own interest. The theory of evolution and our acceptance of the process of natural selection leave us with no option but to suppose that the Arctic tern's best chance of living and of producing chicks next year is to fly down to the edge of Antarctica and fatten up on the abundant krill in those southern seas.

Vertical migrations of species inhabiting mountainous regions can also be interpreted along the same lines; the White-capped Redstart nests up to 12,000 feet in the Himalayas, but afterwards escapes the icy grip of winter by moving several thousand feet lower into the more hospitable foothills. Similarly, in Europe, the insectivorous Wall-creeper with its gorgeous red epaulets may descend into the valleys where the hunting is easier during the winter.

For many birds, migration does not necessarily involve tremendously long flights. For instance, Redwings and Fieldfares – thrushes which breed in the extreme north of Europe – merely move a few hundred or perhaps a thousand miles to escape the worst of the winter in the north of their range. These thrushes invade the British Isles to spend the winter there and take advantage of the mild oceanic climate. Some widely distributed species are also only migratory in parts of their range. Robins and blackbirds are regular migrants in Europe, but the British sub-species of both are more or less sedentary. The less harsh weather conditions have not favoured the evolution of migratory behaviour in the British breeders.

What causes the migration urge?

The factor which triggers off migration is almost certainly the changing hours of daylight. Birds, and many other animals, are extremely sensitive to the changing 'photo period', as it is called. In autumn, the rapidly shortening days bring about an alteration in the birds' hormonal balance which causes them to lay down reserves of fat. Also they become restless, and their character

Penguins migrate across land and ice and wherever possible they slide on their backs – here they have worn deep tracks in the snow descending a steep slope.

changes. Territorial species may become highly sociable, and the massing of swallows in flocks and, in North America, the bobolinks are familiar signs of pre-migratory behaviour.

When weather conditions are suitable, migration begins, and the birds then respond to a set of instructions in their nervous systems, inherited from and perfected by the trial and error of countless generations. Natural selection becomes very rigorous during migration periods. One can imagine that any weaklings among the small land birds in Western Europe which set off on long migratory flights in hostile weather conditions, or in a direction taking them on a hopeless course into the Atlantic, would very quickly be weeded out. Thus we know that in autumn, warblers, chats and flycatchers start their journey south from Scandinavia when anticyclonic conditions prevail over the North Sea, bringing clear skies and light, and favourable, or at least no unfavourable winds. Other weather systems may conceal squawls and gale force head winds over the North Sea, which take a tremendous toll of migrants.

Birds may not be conscious weather prophets, but migration is doubtless triggered off in birds in the migrating mood by a certain favourable combination of external events. These will, of course, vary from species to species and from

place to place. Thus the conditions of wind and sky that send the Snow Geese cackling down the flyways to overwinter in California differ from those which set the Needle-tailed Swifts speeding northwards from Australasia to their breeding grounds.

Tracking migrants

No-one can fail to be inspired by the sight of birds on migration, and it is, therefore, not surprising that ornithologists have devoted a great deal of energy to recording their movements. Many bird observatories are placed at strategic points in the avian flyways. Cap Gris Nez on the northern coast of France is a natural departure point for Passerines leaving the continent of Europe to overwinter in the British Isles. In autumn, vast flocks of starlings and chaffinches can be seen winging their way up into the sky, perhaps in the face of strong westerly winds, to make the Channel crossing; while beneath them thousands of dumpy common scoter, mainly from the Baltic, pass in long lines hugging the wave tops on their

journey westwards. Visible migration over the island of Falstarbo in the Baltic reaches staggering proportions, as chaffinches, bramblings, starlings and raptors flee south before the implacable march of winter.

From direct observations it is possible to map out the major migration routes of certain species. In North America, the famous, and, alas, all too rare Whooping Cranes can be tracked from their breeding grounds in Canada to their wintering quarters in the Aransas wildlife refuge on the edge of the Gulf of Mexico. The flyways that the North American wildfowl use have been largely pieced together by watching and recording the progress of the ducks and geese as they travel from one wetland refuge to another.

A further sophistication of direct observation has come in with the use of high powered radar equipment, which is of tremendous value in monitoring migration. Flocks of birds show up as spots on the screen, or Plan Position Indicator, and for the first time it has been possible to see quite clearly the extent of avian traffic by night. Many species tend

Above, Snow Geese migrate southwards in winter, flying in an attractive 'v' formation.

Right, the endearing Manx Shearwater makes a spectacular journey from Western Europe to Brazil and Argentina, though it cannot rival its close relative the Muttonbird of Tasmania which covers 22,000 miles a year.

to feed during the day and travel only when it is dark, and warblers, thrushes and waders all tend to start their journeys during the evening. It is also quite apparent that the vast majority of birds migrate at heights which render them invisible from the ground. Over England, the most frequent altitude seems to be around 2,700–3,000 feet, although a considerable amount of avian traffic occurs well above this height. Incidentally, a number of species like the Siberian White Crane must regularly cross the Himalayas and reach heights of around 14,000 feet on bi-annual journeys to and from their breeding grounds.

Radar watches have shown how certain land birds, like wheatears and thrushes, tend to lose altitude at night while crossing open sea, and then gain height at dawn. They have even cast some doubt upon the validity of information obtained by ground observation about visible migration. Very often it seems as though the main high altitude bird movements as tracked by radar bear little relation to what ornithologists report from sea level where low flying birds may represent the 'lost' ones that have become disorientated.

Ringing, or bird banding, is perhaps the technique that has been most helpful to us in finding out where birds go when they are migrating. The first large scale ringing scheme was started in 1899 in Denmark and since then millions

Above, Swallows are the traditional sign of summer in Britain, and when they collect in large numbers on the telephone wires in October it means that the cold weather will be coming as soon as the flocks have left.

Right, winter is coming . . . as Starlings take to the air in overwhelming numbers at the start of their journey south.

*Above, migrating Bobolinks were
once notorious crop damagers, as vast
flocks used to stop off at the rice
fields in the Carolinas on their way
to and from Argentina where they
spend the winter. They were killed
in their thousands and the fat
Autumn migrants were sold as
delicacies for gourmets. Their
breeding grounds in the north have
shifted over to the west now that
hayfields are few on the East coast,
but it is interesting that the
migrating birds still follow the old
routes and travel eastwards before
turning south.*

*Right, Redwings are members of the
Thrush family, and look very like
the well-known Song Thrush except
for a blood red patch under each
wing. They usually come south from
their breeding grounds for the winter,
but never travel very far.*

Above, a Common Scoter on its nest. These dumpy sea ducks breed mainly around the Baltic and travel westwards to winter. Rather than travelling at considerable heights, like many species, they hug the waves on their journey.

of birds have been individually tagged. In the British Isles alone, between 1909 and 1968, nearly 6,400,000 birds were ringed and 171,520 recovered. By plotting the recoveries, it is possible to build up a picture of the pattern of dispersal of each species. Occasionally ringing recoveries will provide us with information that it would be impossible to obtain by any other method. For example, the three breeding populations of Barnacle Geese do not intermingle during the winter, but have their separate winter feeding ranges.

How fast?

The other advantage of being able to recognize individuals is that the recoveries provide information on the *speed* at which migrants make their journeys. A Blue-winged Teal ringed in North America has been known to cover at least 3,800 miles in one month, which is an average of 125 miles a day. Even this record is dwarfed into insignificance by the recent report of a Knot (a wading bird) ringed in the British Isles and recovered eight days later, 3,500 miles away, in Liberia.

It seems likely that many species are 'long haul' migrants that are capable of sustaining flight for at least one or two days before refuelling. It is clear that some perching birds must make considerable flights over the sea before reaching land; for example Greenland wheatears, which are larger and rather longer in the wing than the ones nesting on

the mainland of Europe, probably fly directly across 2,000 miles of the North Atlantic in the autumn to make a landfall in Spain. Even the diminuitive Ruby-throated Hummingbird buzzes non-stop for 500 to 1,000 miles across the Gulf of Mexico. The Sahara Desert is probably crossed by many small warblers without resting.

We have already shown that migrating birds can make long distance flights, and some do so from necessity. For instance, the Pacific race of the American Golden Plover flies directly from its Canadian breeding grounds to winter in Hawaii, a journey of 2,000 miles, and one that would do credit to many airliners! Like aircraft, birds need fuel; long haul species like sanderling, curlew, sandpiper and knot accumulate fat before migrating, and it may account for 50% of their body weight when they leave. From what is known about the energy requirements of birds, it has been calculated that one weighing 20 gms. with a maximum load of fat could have a theoretical flight range of between 1,300 and 3,600 miles! Migrants that habitually make their journeys in small stages accumulate lighter loads of body fat; these can 'refuel' en route.

Living Compasses!
Perhaps the most puzzling feature of migration is how birds find their way across the surface of the earth so successfully. Some of the feats of navigation are really quite remarkable; Bristle-thighed Curlews, which nest in the high Canadian

Two Black-browed Albatrosses go through their greeting ceremony as part of their courtship. These birds do not actually migrate, but are quite capable of travelling from one side of the world to the other as often as they please and at remarkable speeds, riding on the strong prevailing winds over the world's oceans. Experiments have shown that they can travel 317 miles a day with ease.

Below, ringing a Hummingbird with a tiny, specially made aluminium band.

tundra, find their way to Tahiti, a mere pin-point in the middle of the Pacific to winter there (see also the case of the Pacific golden plover). Bronze Cuckoos spend their off season on the Solomon and Bismark Islands and undertake a transoceanic flight to New Zealand to breed, despite winds that might throw them off course.

Most people are aware of the feats of homing shown by racing pigeons, but their abilities are nothing compared with the amazing accomplishments of wild birds artificially

released from their nest sites. A Manx Shearwater removed from its burrow on the Welsh island of Skockholm, and released at Boston Airport, made the 3,050 mile flight across the trackless Atlantic to its nest in 12½ days. 18 Layson Albatrosses removed from their nesting quarters on Midway Island in the central Pacific were released at distances up to 4,120 miles away. 14 returned at speeds of up to 317 miles a day! Adelie Penguins have also been taken up to 2,200 miles from their rookery site, to return 10 months

later at an average speed of 8 miles a day.

It is, therefore, quite apparent that birds must have a very accurate means of assessing where they are on the surface of the earth in relation to their home base or destination. Various theories have been put forward over the years – such as, that birds are able to navigate by means of Corioli's Force or by being directly influenced by the earth's magnetic field.

However, a great mass of scientific data has now been accumulated which supports the view that birds use both the sun and the stars as navigation beacons, and this explains why migrants become so disorien-

tated if they run into overcast or foggy conditions. Over twenty years ago it was discovered by Gustav Kramer that during the period of normal migration captive starlings would establish themselves in their cage in the direction they should be travelling in – providing they could see the sun. By a suitable arrangement of mirrors, the apparent position of the sun could be altered, and this was reflected in corresponding changes in the starling's position. An adelie penguin acted in the same way when released on the featureless wastes of Antartica. While the sun was visible, it set out on an accurate NNE course, but as soon as the sun was obscured, its movement became

random, and it was confused.

Of course, much migration takes place at night and again, it seems that celestial clues are used. Captive blackcaps and garden warblers flutter predominantly in SW and NE directions in the autumn and spring respectively, providing they can see a part of the clear night sky. The pattern of 'fixed' stars provide the clues, a fact substantiated by placing birds in planetaria. When the appropriate night sky was projected, the birds orientated themselves in the right migrating direction. Then as the star pattern changed to another sky appropriate to a point where the species are known to be likely to change direction, the birds

Above, a pack of about 5,000 Knot waiting for the right weather before travelling south, and left, a Blue-winged Teal. Both these species cover enormous distances in very short periods of time.

accordingly altered their course.

In order to use celestial clues, birds must have an accurate sense of timing to make allowances for the change in direction of the sun or stars as the day or night progresses. It would seem that they possess an internal biological clock. With their extremely sensitive vision, it is likely that by watching the sun for a very short period, a species like the manx shearwater can compute the highest point on the arc (i.e. its position at midday). When the bird is removed from its home base, the comparison between the highest elevation of the sun at the point of release and at the home base will give information about the bird's relative latitude.

If the sun is too high then it must fly north; if it is too low then it must strike out to the south. Information about its longitudinal position will be revealed by its biological clock. If the sun appears to be too far on its daily course across the sky at any given moment, the bird must be too far west in relation to its home base, and so on.

Migration is an infinitely more subtle business than flying on a fixed heading. Many migration routes are far from straight and the air is rarely still, and birds must be able to compensate for drift. Experience also counts for something; the adults which have already made the journey may possibly remember

certain land marks, and may even be able to reorientate more successfully when they have drifted off course; on the other hand the juveniles of migrating species can take up the appropriate course without apparent trouble. Several thousand starlings were trapped in Holland while migrating SW, and they were ringed and released several hundred miles away in Switzerland. The results were very interesting; the immature birds continued headlong on their SW course and were recovered in SW France and Spain, while the adults apparently reorientated NW and thus compensated for their displacement. Next spring, the immatures apparently returned to the area of their birth, but in subsequent years, they continued to overwinter in SW France and Spain!

Some young birds, like cuckoos and sharp-tailed shearwaters from Australia, can get no guidance from the adults because they have gone on ahead of their offspring. This is precisely what makes migration so fascinating. Many migratory birds have a brain that can sit comfortably on a thumb nail, and yet when only a few months old can expedite journeys of fantastic proportions and can, with such apparent expertise, reach places of which they cannot have had any prior knowledge or experience.

Above, all the Sandpipers except for a few Snipe breed in the Northern Hemisphere and travel tremendous distances every year to opposite ends of the globe.

Right, American Golden Plovers nest in the Alaskan Tundra and winter in southern South America, travelling south down the Atlantic coast and north up the Mississippi valley.

Birds of South-east Asia, Australia and New Zealand

MALCOLM ELLIS

From India eastwards across tropical Asia and down through the Philippines, Borneo, the Celebes and the Greater and Lesser Sunda Islands east to Timor live a rich variety of birds, many of them extremely colourful and abundant, while others, particularly pheasants, struggle to exist as the human population rapidly expands. Many barbets as well as woodpeckers, parrakeets and broadbills live in the forests of this area, while leafbirds occur nowhere else. The bird life changes somewhat from eastern Indonesia eastwards to New Guinea, Australia, New Zealand and Polynesia, where such birds as the cassowaries, megapodes, lyrebirds, cockatoos, birds of paradise and bowerbirds are more characteristic.

The Common or Blue Peafowl (*Pavo cristatus*), of which white, pied, and black-shouldered mutations are to be seen in captivity, is a native of India and Ceylon. It is commonly seen in zoos and on many country estates – it has been kept as an ornamental bird for over 2,000 years – and is too well known to warrant a description. By no means as familiar is the Green Peafowl (*P. muticus*), which inhabits Burma, Thailand, Indochina and Java, and differs from the former mainly in that the male, or peacock, is chiefly green. The long ornamental feathers which form the train are not, as is often supposed, the peacock's tail feathers but are elongated feathers growing from the base of the tail.

Fairy-bluebirds, ioras and leafbirds, which are usually clumped together under the latter name, are a small group and are particularly numerous in Malaysia. They are close to the bulbuls as well as the drongos and cuckoo-shrikes. The two species of fairy-bluebirds are forest dwellers that feed mostly on berries, especially the small wild figs of banyans. Found in India, Burma, Thailand, Indochina, Malaysia and Palawan, the male Blue-backed Fairy-bluebird (*Irena puella*) is light iridescent blue and velvety black with a ruby red eye.

The leafbirds proper are principally green, with black, orange or blue on the head and throat. They feed on fruit, berries and insects, and are also fond of flower nectar and pollen. Called fruitsuckers by most aviculturalists, the Golden-fronted Leafbird (*Chloropsis aurifrons*) and Orange-bellied Leafbird (*C. hardwickii*) are two species that are popular cage birds.

The Great Hornbill (*Buceros bicornis*), occurring from India to Sumatra, is one of the largest and most striking members of its family, which is widely distributed in the Old World tropics. Hornbills are odd looking creatures, whose bills are sometimes given an absurd appearance by the addition of an extra piece on top, called a casque. Their plumage lacks bright colours and is predominantly black, brown and

High in the mountains from the Himalayas across to Indo China and Formosa live a number of breathtakingly beautiful Pheasants which are now frequently seen in zoos. This is a male Golden Pheasant – his wings are brilliant blue and green and the flowing feathers over the back and top of the tail are bright gold.

Left, an Indian Roller sits on a prominent perch waiting to dart out and seize a passing locust or butterfly as is their fashion. They get their name from their tumbling and wheeling flight when excited.

Below, another beautiful Pheasant from Formosa which is called Swinhoe's Pheasant and can easily be kept in captivity.

Above, a Great Hornbill from the Old World Tropics . . . these birds can hardly be called beautiful, but they have many interesting features and habits. For instance, they are the only birds to have such well developed eye lashes, and they have an amazing repertoire of roars, grunts, whistles and bellows in addition to the chuffing noise made by the wind in their wings when they fly.

Left, one of the best known and most beautiful birds of all, the Peacock, which in the wild is a native of India and Ceylon.

Above, a Rainbow Bee-eater landing with a beakful of food outside its burrow. These jewel-like birds spend their time darting gracefully after insects and are strictly arborial except in the breeding season. They dig tunnels sometimes up to two feet in length in sandbanks before laying their eggs in a chamber at the end.

Right, the curly crest and fluffy feathers belong to the Sulphur-crested Cockatoo.

Left, an Australian Rosella.

white, brighter hues usually being confined to the bill and casque, but in some larger species the skin around the eye and the wattles hanging from the throat may also be brightly coloured.

The hornbill's casque, like the toucan's bill, is not as heavy as it may appear, for it too is usually filled with a honeycomb-like material. An exception is the casque of the Helmeted Hornbill (*Rhinoplax vigil*), which is solid and has a consistency similar to elephant ivory. In ancient times these casques, deep red on the outside and golden yellow inside, were prized imports into China where only the finest craftsmen were permitted to carve them.

Hornbills nest in holes or hollows in trees, sometimes but not always at a great height from the ground, and with the exception of the African ground hornbills the female is walled into the nesting chamber, leaving just a slit through which the male can pass food to her. The entrance

is filled with dung and other materials that set hard. Smaller species normally lay three to five eggs and the larger species two, or even only one. While imprisoned in the nesting hole, the female and later the offspring are safe from predators, and during this time the female takes the opportunity to undergo a moult, shedding her flight and tail feathers and replacing them with fresh ones.

Yearly, huge numbers of nestling hill mynahs are imported into Europe and the United States from south-east Asia, particularly India. Chiefly black with a purple, blue and green sheen, a yellow-orange bill and yellow wattles on the head and neck, mynahs are not in demand so much for their looks as for their wonderful ability to imitate the human voice. The Greater Hill Mynah (*Gracula religiosa intermedia*), which is the most frequently kept race, often learns to 'talk' far more clearly than most parrots. In their natural habitat mynahs are

Above, the Kookaburra is the most famous Australian bird and is often referred to as the 'bushman's clock' from the loud raucous chorus the birds give at dusk and dawn.

Right, a Muttonbird feeding its fluffy, brown chick. These young birds are captured from the coasts of Tasmania in large numbers and are canned and eaten as Tasmanian 'Squab' while their down is used in sleeping bags and their stomach oil in cosmetics and drugs.

strictly arboreal, seldom descending to the ground, and feed on wild fruits.

The closely related Indian Mynah (*Acridotheres tristis*) has been introduced into such countries as Australia and New Zealand and has multiplied so rapidly in Hawaii that it has become a pest. Another Asiatic bird introduced into Australia and New Zealand is the Spotted Dove (*Streptopelia chinensis*).

Rollers, bee-eaters, and kingfishers are three very colourful groups well represented from India through south-east Asia to Australia. Principally various shades of blue, the rollers, who are not as numerous in Asia as Africa, take their name from the habit of somersaulting and rolling during display flights. The Indian Roller (*Coracias benghalensis*), sometimes misleadingly called the Blue Jay, occurs through southern Asia from Arabia to Cambodia. Smaller than the more typical rollers is the Broad-mouthed Dollarbird or Indian Broad-billed Roller (*Eurystomus orientalis*), which feeds on insects caught on the wing. It does not roll or tumble but makes long,

swooping flights. This species occurs from northern India to Manchuria, while the Australian race breeds in the north and east of the continent and migrates to New Guinea and its neighbouring islands.

Another bird that breeds in Australia and then migrates to New Guinea and the Celebes is the Rainbow Bee-eater or Rainbowbird (*Merops ornatus*). The European Bee-eater (*M. apiaster*) breeds as far east as western Siberia and Kashmir, migrating to Africa and north-west India. Bee-eaters inhabit tropical and milder temperate parts of the Old World. They are absent from New Zealand.

The largest concentration of kingfishers is to be found in the islands of south-east Asia, with several including the famous Laughing Kingfisher or Kookaburra (*Dacelo novaeguineae*) occurring in Australia and one in New Zealand. Races of the Pied Kingfisher (*Ceryle rudis*) that is common in Africa are to be found living in Asia, and the Kingfisher (*Alcedo atthis*) of Europe goes as far east as the Solomon Islands. There are a number of small brightly

coloured, mostly insect-eating, three-toed species, two of which extend down to Australia. The only species to occur in New Zealand is the Sacred Kingfisher (*Halcyon sancta*), a bird that is widespread in Australia.

Aptly named, the tailorbirds (*Orthotomus spp.*) construct the most ingenious of nests. Firstly they select two large leaves, then with the bill puncture holes around the edges of them. These small warblers next proceed to collect strands of cottony fluff which they push through the holes in the two leaves, drawing them together. In the little pocket that is thus formed the tailorbird builds its nest from fine grasses and plant down.

It is the nests made by some of the cave swiftlets (*Collocalia spp.*) that are the source of the famous bird's nest soup of the East. Some of these swiftlets build pure white nests composed of salivary secretion. These are the most highly prized of all; others that contain feathers or vegetable matter being less highly prized. The job of collecting the nests from dark caves is usually done

Above, tame Cormorants being trained to fish from leads by a Japanese fisherman.

Left, the magnificent Monkey-eating Eagle from the Phillipines is unfortunately becoming increasingly rare.

by a man with a set of connecting bamboo poles with a blade attached for scraping them from the cave walls.

Cormorants (*Phalacrocorax carbo sinensis* and *P. capillatus*) in the Orient are tamed and trained by fishermen to assist them in their work, a custom which dates back hundreds of years. In Japan, where this method goes back to the sixth century, fishermen operate from a boat with a team of perhaps a dozen birds, each on a leather tether. The cormorants are put into the water and are pulled back aboard just as soon as they have a throat full of fish. A thong is tied around the base of the neck while they are working, so that they are unable to swallow their tasty catch.

China is the home of the beautiful Mandarin Duck (*Aix galericulata*), a species that has been introduced into parts of the Western world. Caged pairs were in the past given as presents at Chinese weddings, as symbols of marital fidelity. Despite its goose-like gait, the Australian Wood Duck or Maned Goose (*Chenonetta jubata*), is probably closely allied to the Mandarin and also the Wood Duck (*A. sponsa*) of North America.

The lovely Golden Pheasant (*Chrysolophus pictus*) and Lady Amherst's Pheasant (*C. amherstiae*), two species well known in captivity, inhabit the mountains of central and

western China. Captive-bred Swinhoe's Pheasants (*Lophura swinhoei*) have recently been released in Taiwan to swell the wild stock that has dwindled to a dangerous level. This bird was first described by John Gould in 1862, yet now over a century later little is known about its range in the hill forests of Taiwan. It may always have been rare. Another endangered species from the same locality is the Mikado Pheasant (*Syrmaticus mikado*).

A magnificent raptor from the Philippines, the huge, fierce-looking Monkey-eating Eagle (*Pithecophaga jefferyi*), with a present population of fewer than 100 birds, seems to have a very bleak future ahead. Its forest abode is being cut down for timber and to make way for cultivation, while among the inhabitants of the Philippines to possess a stuffed mounted eagle has become a status symbol. Zoos fortunately are becoming more conservation conscious, and the better establishments

have decided to import no more of these rare creatures that were once prized exhibits.

New Guinea and its nearby islands is the stronghold of the fabulous birds of paradise renowned for their splendid plumage. Among many males of this group the development of special feathers to attract the opposite sex reaches its peak, for not only do their feathers exhibit an enormous variety of colours, but also an astonishing array of weird and fanciful shapes. As a general rule the most gaily plumaged males have the dullest mates, and pairs are not usually formed; instead, the females visit the males at their display places, mate, then go away to nest and raise their brood independently.

Prior to beginning their display dances, which are performed by a number of birds gathered together among the branches of a tree, male Greater Birds of Paradise (*Paradisaea apoda*) utter a chorus of loud, raucous cries. Then, starting to

Above, the male Lesser Bird of Paradise starting his display . . . the tail plumes are yellow shading to mauve and at the height of the display they are flung over the bird's back in a great fan.

Right, Emus still run across the fields and plains of Australia in large numbers in spite of much persecution in the past.

dance, they gradually become more excited until eventually, leaning forward, they drop their wings and throw their long yellowish flank plumes up over the back. Named after Austria's Crown Prince Rudolph, the male Blue Bird of Paradise (*P. rudolphi*) has blue plumes that flow down either side of his body as he displays hanging upside down from the limb of a tree.

During the early 1900s so many Greater Birds of Paradise were slaughtered for their plumes to satisfy the demands of European and American fashion that it was feared they might become extinct. As a safeguard a number were taken from the Aru Islands and introduced on to Little Tobago in the West Indies, where some of their descendants still survive.

The smaller male King of Saxony Bird of Paradise (*Pteridophora alberti*) possesses two extraordinary wires more than twice the length of the bird, one coming from each side of the head just behind the eye and having a row of small, celluloid-like tabs along one side. Just six inches in body length, the King Bird of Paradise (*Cicinnurus regius*) is the smallest of the family. The mainly red and white male has two sweeping tail wires, tipped with a twist of gleaming green feathers.

Closely akin to the previous group are the bowerbirds, also of New Guinea and Australia. Known as a maypole builder, the dull-plumaged male Gardener Bowerbird (*Amblyornis inornatus*) of New Guinea builds an elaborate structure like a miniature native hut. The structure, which may be three feet high, is built around the base of a small sapling, and the bowerbird earns his name by surrounding it with a garden decorated with flower petals that are renewed almost daily.

A native of eastern Australia, the Satin Bowerbird (*Ptilonorhynchus*

A male Superb Lyre Bird displaying (above) and resting between performances (right). The perfect lyre-shape of the tail feathers which is so well-known from Australian postage stamps only exists for a few seconds as the bird flings the feathers up over his head at the climax of his display. The outer tail feathers which form the frame of the lyre can be seen clearly on the right and are strikingly banded and curved and have round black tips. The inner feathers consist only of quills and have a delicate, lacy look in consequence. The space in the undergrowth that the bird has cleared to dance on is quite plain on the left.

violaceus) is a larger bird about the size of a Jackdaw. The glossy, purplish-blue male builds an avenue made from thousands of small twigs stuck upright into a patch of clear ground. He then decorates the avenue, called a bower, with blue objects of similar shade to rival males, and paints it with masticated fruit-pulp.

Prince Albert's Lyrebird (*Menura alberti*) and the Superb Lyrebird (*M. superba*) are also native to eastern Australia and have no near relatives anywhere, the closest birds probably being the Western or Noisy Scrub-bird (*Atrichornis clamosus*) (which was sighted again in 1961 after having been thought extinct) and the Rufous Scrub-bird (*A. rufescens*). The smaller of the two lyrebirds is Prince Albert's, which lives in a relatively small area of dense rain forest in north-east New South Wales and south-west Queensland, where it is sometimes heard but only rarely seen. The Superb species has been closely studied, mainly near Sydney and in Sherbrooke Forest near Melbourne, where it is fairly numerous.

It is known to be a fine songster, a brilliant mimic, and to perform a most impressive display, for which it may clear as many as ten or more circular areas in the forest undergrowth. Each of these clearings made by the male is about three feet in diameter and is slightly raised above the ground. The male lyrebird may display several times a day, at the climax of which he brings his wonderful tail feathers up over his head and allows them to cascade before him. At the same time he prances about, singing his own notes, as well as imitating those of a wide variety of other birds. Mimicry has been developed to an extraordinary extent by these birds and their repertoire may include the calls not only of other birds but also mammals, together with such sounds as the whine of a circular saw, the hoot of a car horn, or the whistle of a railway engine.

Exceeded in size only by the Ostrich, the Emu (*Dromaius novae-hollandiae*) stands between five and six feet tall and rarely weighs more than 100 pounds. It occurs over most of the continent except in the tropical north-eastern corner where

it is replaced by the Australian Cassowary (*Casuarius casuarius*). Emus are treated as a serious pest in many places, particularly in wheat growing country where they trample crops and knock down fences. Huge numbers have been killed over the years, but nevertheless this bird continues to flourish. Normally it lays eight to ten green eggs on a bed of trampled down grasses, bark and leaves placed below a tree or bush, and despite the eggs' size and colour they are surprisingly difficult to find. They are laid in the autumn and are incubated by the male alone for 58–61 days. When they hatch out the chicks are pale grey in colour, with conspicuous black and yellow stripes. Emus only begin to breed in their second year.

A distinctive feature of the cassowaries is the bony helmet or casque on top of the bare head, which is used to ward off obstructions as the birds run through thick undergrowth in their rain forest habitat. The skin of their unfeathered heads and necks combines reds, blues, purple and yellow, while some also have decorative wattles hanging from the neck. Cassowaries, which are black, have stout powerful legs, and the innermost of the three toes is armed with a long sharp claw. They can be aggressive, and in combat leap feet first at an adversary. There are many records of them killing human beings when cornered, mostly in New Guinea, but there has also been at least one European boy killed in Queensland.

Whereas nearly all birds incubate their eggs with their own body heat, the megapodes lay theirs in holes in the ground or in mounds of rotting vegetation, allowing them to be hatched by natural heat. A small group, they are confined to eastern Indonesia, Polynesia, New Guinea, and Australia, with the exception of one species. Members of the group are known by such names as scrub-fowl and brush-turkeys, while one is called the Mallee Fowl (*Leipoa ocellata*) and others junglefowl, a name more correctly applied to the group from which our domestic fowl have descended. Mound-birds, mound-builders and incubator birds are general terms used to describe the group as a whole.

Brush-turkeys, which are black

with a bare head and neck, all build mounds chiefly of plant material, commonly about twelve feet in diameter and three feet high. In the warm, moist jungles the mounds ferment rapidly and generate considerable heat. Other species simply lay their eggs in a hole dug on a beach or sandy soil exposed to the sun. They fill in the hole and never visit the site again.

Almost exclusively a bird of dry scrub in inland Australia, the Mallee Fowl or Lowan, is the only megapode to inhabit semi-arid country. In such places where leaf mould does not form and fallen leaves quickly dry and wither, the bird digs a hole in the ground that may be 15 feet in diameter and three or four feet deep. During the winter it fills the hole with vegetable matter that, once it has been dampened by a shower of rain, is covered with a layer of sandy soil. Cut off from dry air the matter ferments and starts to generate heat, which later is supplemented by solar heat.

The number of eggs laid by Mallee Fowl varies from five to thirty five. Throughout the incubation period, which extends from September to March or April, the male tends the mound, keeping the temperature at around 32° C by increasing or decreasing the insulating layer of soil. Either building or maintaining the mound keeps the male bird busy for eleven months of the year. The eggs are laid over a period of several months, so that the earliest eggs have hatched and the chicks departed before the last are laid. Upon breaking out of the eggshell the chicks dig their way out of the mound without any help, and run off into the scrub alone.

First brought alive from Australia in 1840 by the remarkable scientist and artist John Gould, the popular Budgerigar (*Melopsittacus undulatus*) is just one of many members of the parrot family which abound in this part of the world. Naturally their plumage is green, but by selective breeding in captivity a great variety of other colours has been evolved. Several of the Australian parrakeets or rosellas (*Platycerus spp.*) and their allies are clad in gorgeous greens, yellows, reds and blues; while cockatoos, which are

Left, the Mallee Fowl is one of the Megapodes which build a large heap of sand in which to incubate their eggs. The male Mallee Fowl has a heat sensitive lining to his beak which enables him to test the temperature of the soil and keep the heat even.

Above, the extraordinary casque of the Cassowary is thought to be a protection as the birds move through the undergrowth. The featherless head and neck are often brilliantly coloured in reds, blues and yellows.

restricted chiefly to New Guinea and Australia, are mostly white and pink, or black. Found from eastern Indonesia to north Queensland and the Solomons, the Eclectus Parrot (*Lorius roratus*) exhibits particularly marked sexual dimorphism, for the male is green and the female red and blue. Native to New Guinea and its adjacent islands, the pygmy parrots (*Micropsitta spp.*) do not exceed four inches in length and are the smallest of all the parrots.

The strange, aberrant Magpie Goose (*Anseranus semipalmata*) has long orange legs with elongated toes that are only slightly webbed, and unlike most other waterfowl moults its flight feathers progressively instead of all at once, so that it is at no time flightless. It seems likely that this bird may form some kind of link with the South American screamers. One of three species of swans living

in the Southern Hemisphere, the Black Swan (*Cygnus atratus*), with its sooty black plumage and red bill, has been introduced from its native Australia into New Zealand, which is also the home of the New Zealand Shelduck (*Tadorna variegata*). A large grey bird, the Cape Barren or Cereopsis Goose (*Cereopsis novae-hollandiae*) is confined to a very few Australian islands, where it is probably declining.

Smallest of the penguins is the Little or Fairy Penguin (*Eudyptula minor*), a species that is to be found on the coasts and islands of southern Australia from Perth to Brisbane, around Tasmania, New Zealand, and the Chatham Islands. The Rock-hopper Penguin (*Eudyptes crestatus*), which has yellow plumes coming from above the eyes and falling down the sides of the head, breeds in New Zealand as well as Tristan

Above, the supremely elegant Black Swan of Australia.

Right, the Flightless Rail of New Zealand was thought to be extinct and was then rediscovered. The birds have since been carefully protected.

da Cunha, Gough Island, the Falkland Islands and various islands of the Antarctic, while the Fiordland Crested Penguin (*Eudyptes pachyrhynchus*) is restricted to New Zealand, as is the White-flippered species (*Eudyptula albosignata*).

Mention New Zealand to most people and the first thing they will think of is the kiwi, for nothing is more closely associated with this far corner of the Commonwealth than this flightless bird with its long bill and short, stout legs. There are, in fact, not one but five kiwis: the Common Kiwi (*Apteryx australis australia*) occurs on the South Island, where in the west and south the Great Spotted or Large Grey Kiwi (*A. haasti*) and the Little Spotted or Little Grey Kiwi (*A. oweni*) also appear, while *A. a. mantelli* occurs on the North Island, and *A. a. lawryi* on Stewart Island.

For many years after the arrival of Europeans these birds were unnoticed, as during the day they remain hidden, emerging only at night to forage for earthworms, insects, and fallen berries. Kiwis are the only birds to have their nostrils located at the tip of the bill, and because of this they probably have a keen sense of smell, which most other birds lack. Their hearing is also good, while their small eyes suggest that their sight is poorly developed. Today, although their forest home has been greatly reduced they are still plentiful in suitable localities, yet are shy, retiring birds, seldom seen by human beings.

The extinct giant moas probably vanished from New Zealand not too long ago, for they were well known to the Maoris. Although they were probably most closely related to the kiwis, the moas are thought to have looked like huge emus, with the largest, *Dinornis maximus*, towering some ten feet or more above the ground.

For half a century the Flightless Rail or Takahe (*Notornis mantelli*) was thought to be extinct, until some were found in 1948 living on the South Island. Since then they have been studied and carefully protected, so that now there are maybe 200 to 300 birds existing in small scattered groups. The rail's future should be safe, but that of many other New Zealand species, such as the Piopio or Native Thrush (*Turnagra capensis*), the Laughing Owl (*Sceloglaux albifacies*), and the strange, almost flightless Kakapo or Owl Parrot (*Strigops habroptilus*), are endangered. A nocturnal creature, the parrot stays hidden during the day in rock crevices or burrows in beech forests situated in inaccessible and seldom visited places. The Kea (*Nestor notabilis*), a dull olive-brown parrot, is reputed to kill sheep by tearing away the wool on the animals' backs to peck at the fat and flesh.

Discovered on Captain Cook's second voyage, the New Zealand Shore Plover (*Thinornis novaeseelandiae*) once occurred on both the North and South Islands, but is now probably confined just to Rangatira in the Chatham Islands, where it is doing quite well. Another small plover, the Wrybill (*Anarhynchus frontalis*), possesses a curious black beak which curves to the right, a unique adaptation for probing under stones for food. This species breeds on the South Island and migrates to the North Island.

Probably in return for keeping their underground homes free from insects, two shearwaters (*Puffinus carneipes* and *P. bulleri*) that occur in New Zealand share their burrows with the Tuatara. The birds occupy it first, then allow the lizard to share it.

Seabirds

DAVID SAUNDERS

Although the world's oceans cover some 70% of the surface of the globe they are inhibited by only 285 species of seabirds belonging to four different Orders. This contrasts with the 8,600 species of land bird which belong to twenty eight different Orders. Even among those classed as seabirds there are some which are decidedly non-maritime in their habits, such as some of the pelicans and certain members of the gull family.

The small number of seabird species certainly contain a wealth of interest both to the marine ornithologist and the casual observer. There is also the added attraction that to study the birds one often has to travel to remote places, maybe a tropical island, northern fjords, or Polar regions. Their ranks include some of the rarest members of our avifauna, birds on the brink of extinction; while other species are so numerous that their colonies are uncountable, or measured in hundreds of thousands. There are large species and small, some are nocturnal when ashore, others make huge migrations, while some do not stray far from their natal colony.

There is an increasing interest in seabirds at the moment. Some people study them through ringing schemes, or by systematic counts as they pass particular headlands on migration. Others endeavour to learn more about distribution at sea, an aspect which, not surprisingly in

view of the difficulties involved, we know little about. Breeding season surveys are now being carried out more regularly and provide information concerning population trends. In Great Britain and Ireland a particularly important survey – 'Operation Seafarer' was organized by the Seabird Group during 1969/70, when some 1,000 volunteer observers took part. All twenty four species of seabirds breeding in these islands were included, and the results provide a basic source of information against which future changes can be measured, and as such will be of great value to conservationists.

Except for those members of the gull family which scavenge around our towns, the seabird with which most people are familiar is without question the penguin. No zoo can afford to be without a small colony for they have an instant appeal, perhaps due to their human characteristics of an upright stance and inquisitive nature.

There are some eighteen species of penguin, Order *Spheniscidae*, all restricted to the southern hemisphere, though not, as is often thought, wholly to the regions of pack ice and the great ice barriers. Some occur much further north in Australasian, South African and South American waters. In the cool waters of the Humbolt Current the Galapagos Penguin (*S. mendiculus*) thrives within a degree and a half of

Left, a Kittiwake alighting at its nest. These birds have in recent years been nesting inland and on man-made sites and proving themselves able to thrive in such conditions.

the Equator off Ecuador.

The largest species as befits its name is the Emperor (*Aptenodytes forsteri*), standing nearly four feet high and weighing up to sixty five pounds. They nest in the middle of the Antartic night, and a journey to one of their colonies by three members of Scott's last expedition has been aptly described 'as the weirdest birds nesting expedition ever made', and was certainly the most arduous. At the other end of the scale is the fifteen inch high Fairy or Little Blue Penguin (*Eudyptula minor*), a familiar bird to coastal residents of parts of southern Australia, since their nests are often found in cavities beneath coastal bungalows.
Having lost their powers of flight

long ago, the penguin's wings are flattened to form strong, narrow flippers capable of propelling the bird through the water at speeds of up to ten knots. The feathers are short and dense to protect the bird against the cold, and even on the Emperor Penguin do not exceed three and a half inches in length, while on some smaller species they are barely an inch.

Even the penguins living in the Polar regions are by no means safe from man's activities. The development of tourism in this area means that colonies are likely to be disturbed at the critical stages of the breeding cycle. More alarming still are the reports showing the discovery of toxic chemical residues in the

Above, Fairy Penguins are the smallest of all Penguins and are popular birds in Australia as they often build their nests along the beaches and beside coastal houses.

An Emperor Penguin supervises the 'creche' of young birds gathered together on the sea ice. All Penguins nest in vast colonies, and it is the male Emperor Penguins who starve for six weeks while incubating the one egg on top of their feet. The females return from the sea to take over the rearing of the chick and then both parents go off to the sea periodically leaving the young birds to band together in tight groups for protection against predators.

*Right, a Gannetry in Canada . . .
These beautiful birds are spectacular
divers, plunging with a great splash
into the sea from a height of several
hundred feet.*

*Below, a very handsome Rockhopper
Penguin showing the short dense
feathers typical of all Penguins.
They are so called because of their
hopping, shuffling gait on land.*

Above, a Fulmar or Giant Petrel. The picture shows very clearly the peculiar nostril formation which is common to all members of the Tubenosed family.

Above, a male Frigate Bird displaying. This aerial seabird has a scarlet throat pouch which he inflates to an enormous size in the breeding season. He chooses a nest site and then sits solemnly beside it inflating his pouch and waiting for a female to join him.

Left, Tropicbirds are true ocean birds found only in the Tropical seas, and are graceful and attractive white birds with two very long central tail feathers. Sailors have nicknamed them 'bo's'n-birds', though they rarely follow ships.

body tissues of some birds. On the credit side there is the recent colonization of new areas by the Chinstrap Penguin (*P. antartica*), which is thought to be due to the increasing amounts of 'krill', the shrimp-like *crustacea* on which both whales and penguins feed. This is probably due to the decreasing number of whales in the southern oceans. Off the coast of South-West Africa the expansion of the fishing industry could seriously affect the colonies of the Black-footed Penguin (*S. demerus*) by diminishing their food supply, and the same could occur to the Peruvian Penguin (*S. humboldti*) off South America.

Of all the seabirds the albatrosses and the petrels, which both belong to the Order *Procellariiformes*, are

perhaps the most pelagic. Only visiting land to breed, they spend the rest of the year out to sea, some making quite remarkable trans-oceanic migrations. In size they range from the Wandering Albatross (*Diomedea exulans*) which has a wing span of twelve feet, to the Least Storm Petrel (*Halocyptera microsoma*), which is barely five inches in length.

The thirteen species of albatross are for the most part restricted to the southern hemisphere, with three occurring in the North Pacific. Of these the Short-tailed Albatross (*D. albatrus*) is now one of the rarest birds in the world. It breeds on the islands south of Japan and its numbers have been reduced to a mere handful of pairs by fishermen and

feather hunters, and also by volcanic activity.

Although fossil remains of extinct species have been discovered both in England and eastern North America, few birds of the existing species ever visit the North Atlantic. Colonization of this area is prevented by the North American land mass and by the area of mid Atlantic calms known as the Doldrums. This forms an almost insurmountable barrier to these long winged birds which can only make prolonged flights with the aid of air currents. That albatrosses can survive once they reach the North Atlantic is demonstrated by the lone bird that lived amongst the Gannets at Mykines Holm in the Faroes from 1860–94, and more recently by one which has frequented the Bass Rock, Scotland, since 1967.

The twenty-two species of storm petrels are distributed throughout the world's oceans, and two breed in European waters, the British Storm Petrel (*Hydrobates pelagicus*) and Leach's Petrel (*Oceanodroma leucorhoa*). The former has been seen on islands from Iceland to northern Spain, and in the western Mediterranean, and its world range is completed by colonies in the Canaries. Leach's Petrel has a much wider distribution, and is found on many islands in the North Pacific and on the east coast of North America from southern Labrador to Massachussetts. In Europe there are only a handful of colonies, at the Westmann Islands, Iceland, in the Faroes, and at the Flannan Islands, North Rona and Sula Sgeir off north-west Scotland.

Although few ornithologists may be fortunate to visit their European breeding colonies, there are times when Leach's Petrels are blown ashore, sometimes in large numbers. These 'wrecks' occur as the birds disperse slowly southwards during October and encounter prolonged periods of severe westerly winds. Unable to fly against the wind and weakened due to a virtual inability to feed in the rough seas, the birds are inexorably driven eastwards. In extreme conditions many will eventually be cast ashore to die along the strand line. The last severe 'wreck' occurred during the autumn of 1952

Above, Little Auk come near to
rivalling Puffins as the most amusing
birds of the Alcid family. They breed
in the far north and migrate
southwards to both coasts of the
Atlantic.

Top left, the Fairy Prion nests in the
Bass Strait and off New Zealand,
and is blue grey in colour with white
underparts.

Below left, two King Penguins with
immaculate white shirt fronts. They
are very similar to the Emperor
Penguins, though slightly smaller.

when nearly 7,000 were found in
Great Britain and Ireland, and smaller numbers elswhere in western
Europe, including some as far east
as Switzerland.

The *Procellaridae* is a large and
varied family and can be divided
into four main groups. Six heavily
built species are usually classed as
fulmars, five of which are only found
in the higher latitudes of the southern hemisphere, while the sixth,
the Northern Fulmar (*Fulmarus
glacialis*), occurs in both the North
Pacific and North Atlantic. In European waters it has undergone an
intriguing increase. Prior to 1878 it
only nested on St Kilda in the
Flannan Islands in the whole of
Great Britain and Ireland but in that
year it commenced colonization of
the great cliffs of Foula, Shetland.
Since then it has occupied virtually
every sea cliff in Great Britain and
Ireland, an expansion that has been
studied in some detail by ornitholo-

gists. James Fisher, whose name is
synonomous with that of the Fulmar,
considers the increase was initiated
during the era of the Arctic whaling
industry, when large amounts of
offal on which the birds feed became
available. Later the fishing fleets also
produced waste fish on which the
birds gorged themselves. Some
scientists dispute this theory, but
whatever the cause the expansion
of the Northern Fulmar is one of the
success stories of the avian world.

The prions are a group of twelve
species and subspecies found mainly
on sub-Antartic islands where they
nest in rock crevices and in burrows.
The birds feed on zooplankton
found in the sea by straining the
water through their bills with a
comb-like structure called lamellae.
This is carried out as the birds
swim with their heads dipped beneath the surface and wings up-
raised.

The gadfly petrels include among

their number one of the rarest seabirds in the world, the Cahow
(*Pterodoma cahow*) of Bermuda.
They were once numerous, but
sailors and the early settlers rapidly
laid the colonies waste so that eventually the bird was considered extinct. During the early years of the
present century there were occasional reports of an unusual petrel
and eventually this was identified as
the Cahow. However not until 1951
was a breeding colony discovered.
In 1967 twenty two pairs reared
eight young and the total world
population was estimated to be about
80 birds. The birds have not only to
contend with natural predators but
it is thought that in recent years their
low nesting success may be due to
contamination by DDT of the zooplankton on which they feed.

Some members of the shearwater
group are great ocean travellers,
nesting in one hemisphere and moving north or south to the other
during the winter season. One of the
most spectacular voyages is that
undertaken by the Short-tailed
Shearwater (*Puffinis tenuirostris*)
which nests on islands off south-
eastern Australia. Leaving the colonies during late April the birds head
initially north-east before turning
north-west to reach Japan, and one
bird ringed in Tasmania made the
5,500 mile journey in a month. From
Japan the birds head east across the
North Pacific to Alaska, and then
coast southwards before turning
east to reach the breeding grounds
by late September. The whole
20,000 mile figure of eight journey
is made along the direction of

*Above, an Arctic Skua, or Parasitic
Jaeger in light phase colouring. These
are piratical birds which breed round
the North Pole and migrate to
sometimes well south of the Equator,
and are easily identified by the two
elongated central tail feathefs.*

*Right, a Sandwich Tern feeding its
young. These birds are found along
the coast of America and Europe,
though their numbers have dropped
dramatically in Holland which used
to be their main stronghold.*

prevailing ocean winds.

The four species of diving petrel, although belonging to the *Procellariiformes*, are quite unlike the rest of the Order. They have stubby bodies, short necks and wings and are generally restricted to coastal waters. Occurring in the southern hemisphere they occupy the ecological niche which in the north is occupied by the Little Auk or Dovekie (*Plattus alle*), which they closely resemble.

The Order *Pelecaniformes* has five families which are usually considered seabirds, though in the case of the pelicans only the Brown Pelican (*Pelecanus occidentalis*) may be considered maritime.

The cormorant and shag family contains some thirty species, one of which, the Guanay Cormorant (*Phalacrocorax bougainville*), has been described as the most valuable wildbird in the world. They nest on the islands off Peru and Chile and have deposited vast quantities of droppings or guano, which is a valuable nitrogenous fertilizer, over hundreds of years. There has been little erosion in the virtually rain-free climate and commercial exploitation on a vast scale was undertaken during the last century. Between 1848 and 1875 20,000,000 tons worth £715,000,000 was removed, and several species were threatened with extinction as their nests were destroyed. In more recent times a 'cropping' system has been evolved and efforts made to provide more colony sites even to the extent of making suitable mainland promonotories free from their natural predators, and any interference.

The five species of frigate bird are among the most aerial of all seabirds, like swifts and swallows they spend hours at a time on the wing. With a lack of waterproof plumage together with small feet and reduced webs they are not adapted for life on the surface of the sea. They obtain food by chasing other seabirds until they drop or disgorge their last meal; at other times they will swoop low over a tern colony and grab unguarded chicks and eggs. They fly at such speed that they can catch flying fish leaping from the waves.

The three species of tropic birds seem to be more similar to gulls than to the other members of the *Pelecaniformes*. Their flight, shrill cries, plumage characteristics and the fact that the chicks when hatched

are clothed in down contrasts noticeably with the rest of the Order. The nest site is usually on a cliff or other vantage point which allows easy flight access, for the birds are most clumsy on land due to their short legs and bad balance.

There are nine species of gannet and booby, and they are found on the coasts of all continents save Antarctica. The North Atlantic Gannet (*Sula bassana*) has its headquarters in Great Britain and Ireland and the largest colony is that on St Kilda in the Finnan Islands where in 1959 44,000 pairs nested. Gannets lay but a single egg which is incubated by the heat from their webbed feet, for the birds have no brood patch. The chick on hatching weighs a mere 60 grams but during the next nine weeks increases to 4,500 grams on a rich diet of fish. Finally the adults desert their progeny which make their own way to the sea and learn the art of plunging and diving for food by themselves.

Three species of booby are widespread throughout tropical seas, while the other three are much more restricted, and Abbot's Booby (*S. abboti*) only nests on Christmas Island, Indian Ocean. Some species gather to nest in immense colonies, for instance that of the Red-footed Booby (*S. sula*) on Tower Island, Galapagos, has 140,000 pairs, while one colony of the Peruvian Booby (*S. variegata*) is known to have 356,000 pairs.

The large and diverse Order *Charidiformes* contains five families of seabirds. There are only three species of skimmers or scissor bills and they are found respectively in America, Africa and Asia. They have a quite remarkable bill which is normal in the chicks but rapidly alters as they grow so that the upper mandible is shorter than the lower. The birds fish as their name suggests by flying along scooping up the water with their lower mandible.

The four species of skua are among the most piratical of seabirds. Only three nest in the northern hemisphere while the Great Skua (*Catharacta skua*) nests in both the north and south. They are efficient and dangerous predators at the colonies of other seabirds, stealing eggs and killing chicks and even adult birds. Another favourite habit is to harry smaller seabirds until they drop or disgorge the food which they are carrying. The smallest of the family, the Long-tailed Skua (*Stercorarius longicaudus*) is dependent for successful breeding on the state of the lemming population on the northern tundras where it nests. In good years the clutch of eggs is large while in poor years the birds may not nest at all.

Some forty four species comprise the gull family which is an ubiquitous one found throughout the world. Some like the Common Gull

Right, a Herring Gull or Seagull – one of the most common and well-known birds of all.

Below left, two attractive Rockhopper Penguins obviously engaged in conversation.

(*Larus canus*) are more birds of inland areas than the coast, others like the Kittiwakes (*Rissa tridactyla*) only come ashore to nest, while the Ivory Gull (*Pagophila ebumeus*) forages on the leftovers of Polar Bear kills on the Arctic pack ice.

Of particular interest is the vast increase that has occurred in the numbers of certain gull species during the present century, in particular the Herring Gull (*L. argentatus*) in the North Atlantic. This is possibly due to the vastly increased winter food that is available in the form of rubbish dumps, sewage outfalls and fish docks. The increase can be detrimental to other seabirds, since gulls are predators, both as egg stealers and slayers of chicks and adults, and by sheer weight of numbers they may drive away birds like terns. They would seem to be a potential menace to man as transmitters of disease both to himself and farm stock, and a serious bird strike risk develops wherever they gather on airfields.

The terns are similar to the gulls in that the thirty nine species are distributed throughout the world with the main stronghold being in the Pacific regions. One of their number, the Arctic Tern (*Sterna macrura*), is said to enjoy more hours of sunlight than any other living creature. Nesting in high northern latitudes it moves south at the end of the breeding season to spend several months in equally high southern latitudes. Terns are very susceptible to disturbance by man particularly at the beginning of the breeding season. This means that some colonies, particularly in Europe, can only continue to thrive by their inclusion in nature reserves.

The auk family contains some twenty two species, sixteen of which are only found in the North Pacific. In the North Atlantic there is serious concern regarding the decreasing numbers of Razorbills (*Alca torda*) and Guillemot (*Uria algae*) in the southern colonies. This would seem to be partly due to the birds encountering oil slicks while at sea. Guillemots seem to be the worst affected by this menace as indicated by the beached bird surveys now being carried out in western Europe. The same species were also the main casualties during the Irish Sea seabird 'wreck' in the autumn of 1969. The reason for the 'wreck' is still obscure, but breeding season surveys organized by the Seabird Group during the following summer showed that Guillemots had decreased on average by 27% and Razorbills by 19% throughout the Irish Sea.

The report prepared by the National Environmental Research Council on the Irish Sea seabird 'wreck' draws attention to the fact that although pollution in our seas may not as yet be concentrated enough to directly harm wildlife, it may be an important factor when natural hazards such as rough weather, the rigours of moulting and temporary food shortage weaken the birds' resistance. Clearly we need to know much more not only concerning the numbers and distribution of our seabirds, but also of their general biology if we are to understand the factors affecting these species at the present time.

Acknowledgements

The publishers would like to thank the following individuals and organizations for their kind permission to reproduce pictures in this book:

Associated Freelance Artists   11, 21, 75, 107, 126.

Ardea   8, 9, 12, 14–15 top, 16, 20, 23, 65.

Bruce Coleman   Endpapers, 10, 14–15 bottom, 18, 19, 22, 52, 53, 54, 55, 56, 59, 60, 62, 63, 71, 73, 88, 89, 92, 94, 97, 100, 103, 109, 110, 111, 113, 114, 116, 117–123, 125, 128, 129, 130 top, 131, 135.

Colour Library International   17, 45, 50, 57 top right, 108, 127.

Whitney and Karen Eastman   26, 28, 29, 30, 31, 36, 38–39, 46.

Eric Hosking   2, 6, 17 bottom, 25, 32, 37, 40, 41, 42, 43, 44, 48, 68, 69, 70, 72, 74, 76 bottom, 79, 80, 81, 82, 83, 84, 85, 98, 101, 102, 107, 128, 130 bottom, 132, 133.

Frank Lane   27, 33, 34, 35, 46, 47 bottom, 57, 64, 67, 75, 76, 77, 78, 86, 91, 95, 96 top, 99, 106 top, 112.

The Natural History Photographic Agency   51, 61, 93, 96, 105.

Spectrum   106, 108, 115, 134.

Syndication International   47, 58.